Centre for Finance, Technology and Entrepreneurship

Founded in 2017 in London, CFTE is a global platform for education in Fintech and the future of financial services.

More than 100,000 professionals from 100+ countries have participated in CFTE programmes to accelerate their careers in Fintech and new finance. In addition to London, CFTE is present in Singapore (accredited by Institute of Banking and Finance), Abu Dhabi (Abu Dhabi Global Market Academy), Hong Kong (Cyberport), Malaysia (Asian Banking School), Luxembourg (Luxembourg Academy of Digital Finance Academy with LHOFT) and Budapest (Budapest Institute of Banking).

CFTE's objective is to equip professionals and students with the **skills to thrive in the new world of finance**. This includes online courses and specialisations, leadership training and hands-on extrapreneurship experiences in topics such as Fintech, Open Banking, Digital Payments or Artificial Intelligence.

CFTE courses are designed with the principle of **For the industry, by the industry**. Our courses are taught by senior leaders from fast-growing Fintech companies such as Revolut, Plaid, or Starling Bank, innovative financial institutions such as Citi, DBS or Ping An, tech companies such as Google, IBM or Uber and regulators from MAS, ECB or MNB.

In total, more than 200 CFTE experts provide a global view of what's really happening in this new world of finance.

"In a tech world, we bet on people" is CFTE's motto. Our global community is the core of CFTE. Thanks to an innovative and open mindset, CFTE alumni progress in their careers and help others do the same, with notable alumni leading transformation in their organisations. They also attend events and share advice, tips and job opportunities. CFTE alumni have also made an impact through the world's largest Global Fintech Internship by mentoring over 1,000 students from all over the world.

CFTE believes that the new world of finance will be inclusive, diverse, innovative and will have a positive impact on society and people. This starts with people having the right knowledge and mindset so that no one is left behind. Whether you want to learn, contribute or more generally be part of the new world of financial services, we are looking forward to welcoming you.

Contact

Research team: fintechjobreport@cfte.education
Press: press@cfte.education

Website

Courses: courses.cfte.education
Articles: blog.cfte.education

Preface

Huy Nguyen Trieu
Co-founder of CFTE

Tram Anh Nguyen
Co-founder of CFTE

10 years ago, the nascent Fintech industry was made of young entrepreneurs with big visions of changing financial services. Like any new innovations, a few early adopters were enthusiastic about this new Fintech phenomenon, but many were unconvinced about the impact of new entrants into a regulated industry such as finance. Very few, however, could have predicted that 10 years later the cryptocurrency market would reach almost $3 trillion, or that out of the 10 largest financial institutions in the world, there are only 5 banks left.

The digital transformation of Finance is therefore well underway, with important consequences in business model, value chain, operating model, but most importantly **people**. With the 225 largest Fintech companies employing 300,000 people and hiring 40,000 more, this is an industry that employs almost as many people as the whole financial industry in London (400,000) and hires 4 times more (10,000). For job seekers and students, this represents significant opportunities to join a fast-growing industry with high average salaries.

However, despite these attractive conditions, many Fintech startups still fail to find the right talents, not because of the lack of applicants, but lack of applicants who meet their requirements. On the other hand, many candidates - including those with a strong experience in financial services - find it challenging to even be accepted for interviews. If this mismatch continues, this will slow down the growth of Fintech, and most importantly deprive many professionals and students of good job opportunities.

The Fintech Job Report gives an important understanding of the jobs offered by Fintech companies and the skills that are required in the fast growing industry. It should prove insightful for job seekers and students, but more generally those in the finance industry who want to understand the trends of future jobs.

Preface

Looking ahead, the Fintech Job Report is much more than an analysis of current jobs in the domain of Fintech. It is also a lens into the future of jobs in financial services at large, and gives insights into how the nature of skills is changing, impacting how we educate students and train professionals.

These are important trends that are relevant to not only individuals, but also organisations, governments, regulators and universities.

We would like to thank the CFTE team for their contributions to this project, and the organisations and associations who contributed inputs to this report.

We hope that this Fintech Job Report will help many to understand the employment opportunities in Fintech and we see it as a starting point to encourage more dialogue so that the ecosystem as a whole can benefit from a larger pool of talents.

The Fintech Job Report - Book Edition

The idea to expand the report into a book emerged because CFTE is driven by a mission to create an impact in the Fintech industry by building awareness about the massive opportunities available and corresponding skillsets needed to thrive. For us, the book is a constant work in progress, as we believe the insights must continue to evolve with the industry rather than provide static research. We aim to have a fresh set of comprehensive data to empower the market players with the essential insights. Therefore, more enterprises and revelations will be added, as unicorns sparkle across the globe.

The book will be published and available on Amazon, seeking to donate all our proceeds to Epic Foundation, an amazing organisation supporting youth globally.

Industry thought leaders, innovators and colleagues have given us their comments, views and endorsements to support the book and our work. We would like to use this opportunity to thank them for their thoughts and are delighted to have them as members of our CFTE family.

The Fintech Job Report

CONTENTS

1	About CFTE
3	Preface
6	Foreword
15	Executive Summary
17	Introduction
19	PART 1 The Growth of Fintech Startups
27	PART 2 Fintech as an Employer
31	PART 3 The Jobs in Fintech
45	PART 4 The Skills in Fintech
53	PART 5 Jobs in Fintech and the Required Skills
55	The Ideal Fintech Candidates
67	Engineering Roles
79	IT & Operations Roles
87	Data Science Roles
99	Product Management Roles
107	Design Roles
115	Marketing & Communications Roles
125	Sales & Business Development Roles
133	Partnerships Roles
139	Risk & Compliance Roles
151	Core Business Finance Roles
161	Conclusion
162	Appendix
163	Report Methodology
167	List of Contributors

© 2021 Centre for Finance, Technology and Entrepreneurship. All rights reserved. No part of th s publication may be reproduced or transmitted in any form or by any means, including photocopying and recording, or by any information storage and retrieval system.

Foreword

Andrei Kirilenko
Professor of Finance

This report encapsulates the paradigm shift in Financial Services driven by technology. A significantly valuable analysis of the evolving fintech job market that needs talent to venture beyond traditional finance to grow.

Anna Maj
FinTech Leader & Advisor

Being twenty years in the FS industry, I have been witnessing a reshuffle towards tech-oriented roles as well as a creation of new jobs, e.g. bot trainer. The report is pivotal to understand why we need more diversified talent and a new set of capabilities in FinTech to bridge the skills gap, such as creative thinking, cooperative mindset or adaptability.

Anthony Thomas
Chairman at MoMo

I want to commend CFTE on their pioneering efforts in putting together a much-needed global knowledge base for jobs in fintech. Creating a better shared understanding of talent needs and how to meet them will be an accelerator for the industry to progress.

April Rudin
Founder/CEO of The Rudin Group

One of the silver linings of the pandemic has been the 'great resignation' giving workers of all types new opportunities to work more flexibility and develop new skill sets. This report discusses and outlines these opportunities in a compelling and exciting way.

Foreword

Bradley Leimer
Unconventional Ventures and Co-Author, Beyond Good

If you want to know about the future of financial services and technology, and how these twin forces are changing our global society, you need to understand how the nature of work within the industry is changing. The roles are shifting toward a greater purpose, toward serving a more diverse and inclusive world, and the Fintech Job Report works like a map to show you this future right now.

Caroline Stockmann
Chief Executive, Association of Corporate Treasurers

This is an important report, not only giving insight into the trends in FinTech, but also giving a clear overview of roles in this rapidly developing sector. A must-read for anyone wanting to launch a career in FinTech or indeed understand better the developments that may affect them and their way of working in the future.

Chris Skinner
Commentator and Best-Selling Author

This report is important as it shows the depth and breadth of FinTech as a sector. Specifically, by value, the researchers find that the Top 100 FinTech firms have a value equivalent to a third of the value of the Top 100 banks. That, and this report, cannot be ignored.

Daniel Liebau
Founder, Lightbulb Capital

The Fintech Job Report offers essential insights on the future skills required in financial services. The entire industry is at the edge of being re-invented. The suggestion that design, data and finance skills are at the centre of fintech is exciting, refreshing and to see this in writing is encouraging.

Foreword

Dr. Efi Pylarinou
Global Fintech Influencer

CFTE`s report offers a thorough look at the Fintech ecosystem as an employer. It is very timely, as several of the 200+ Fintech unicorns are more than 10 years old and still growing their stack of offerings. The taxonomy of jobs in the report, offers a valuable perspective of the Fintech employment opportunities.

Prof. Dr. Enrico Molinari
Professor in Economics and Management, University Academy of Fine Arts of Sanremo-Luxury Technopole – e-Campus Group

Fintech is everywhere. From customers' Next New digital & mobile payments habits to BNPL model, from ESG investments until Non-Fungible Token (NFT) working on blockchain for representing digital artwork or real estate assets, we already live in the future of Fintech. The 2022 will reshape the traditional banking mindset and "The Fintech Job Report" will guide us on this incredible journey.

Ericson Chan
Group Information & Digital Officer, Zurich Insurance

While fintech flourishes, the mismatch between supply and demand on fintech talent is increasing. This report gives a succinct yet most comprehensive framework for those who wants to stay current in the fintech world. It is also a blueprint for the industry to develop talent.

Fabian Vandenreydt
Strategic Fintech Advisor

The Fintech environment continues to evolve at a dazzling pace. Like other sectors, it faces an enormous challenge to match diverse talents with a stellar number of job opportunities. I recommend CFTE's Fintech Job Report as comprehensive reference material to tackle the people challenge in Fintech from various perspectives.

Foreword

Gaurav Dhar
CEO, Marshal FinTech Partners

For FinTech people - by FinTech people" is perhaps the best summation of this report by the collective hive-mind that is the CFTE. Nowhere else will you find the most current and elaborate sources of information put together to guide you for years to come in the industry.
A must for those who will use this to navigate their way through the ever expanding FinTech world.

Gergely Fabian
CEO of the Budapest Institute of Banking & Executive Director of the Central Bank of Hungary

Unique and superb insight into fintechs from human resources perspective and generally how jobs are evolving in finance. Recommended to people who has opinion about fintechs, so basically to everybody in the world of finance.

Gillian Cribbs
Leadership Coach, Organisational Psychologist and CFTE Advisory

The Fintech Job Report shines a much-needed light on this rapidly growing industry, identifying a groundbreaking taxonomy of new roles in Fintech in addition to key industry trends. Crucially, it will inspire a more diverse range of Fintech hopefuls, encouraging those with the right mindset, soft skills and knowledge to embrace the industry.

Janos Barberis
Co-Founder SuperCharger Ventures

This is the first comprehensive research and analysis of the impact of FinTech on the job market. It is fascinating to read the extent to which financial technology and the billions of investment following it is driven, and will continue to be driven by human capital.

Foreword

Jean - Philippe Desbiolles
Managing Director - Financial Services - IBM Corporation

AI & Data as game changer of the Financial Services Industry. We are in a redefinition of the collaboration between Human and Machine which require new skills, behaviors, aptitudes and potentially new rules to take advantage of it. Tech is not only an enabler but one of the key change factor. This is what we try to bring in this study paper to put things in perspective and allow professionals to project themselves and their organisation in this new era. Technology for sure but Human first. This is the way CFTE continue to progress, I'm honored to bring my contribution. Have a nice reading.

Lex Sokolin
Head Economist, ConsenSys and Founder, Fintech Blueprint

The last decade has profoundly changed how people consume financial products. This seminal report helps us better understand the change in how and by whom the new digital finance is manufactured. It is pivotal reading for anyone looking to transition into fintech professionally, or for builders architecting new teams and organizations in the age to come.

Prof. Lisa Short
Founder, Digital Technology Intellect, Development, Research & Pre-Eminence

Digitisation and technology are advancing so rapidly that changes that once took centuries now happen in years or months. The changes are disrupting political, economic, and social systems as well as cultural norms and social roles. New skills and knowledge about fintech, blockchain, data, and a culture of learning agility give humans an advantage over rapid change and technology. This Fintech Job Report highlights the importance of mastering these skills so people can have the capacity and the skills that enables freedom of passage throughout the world they live and work in, and to build their future of work and learning to positively impacting daily life, community, business, and economic inclusion.

Makoto Shibata
Head of FINOLAB

The FinTech Job Report is very extensive and it is not only for job seekers but also for top management in FinTech startups to plan optimal structure of the organization.

Foreword

Marianne Haahr
Executive Director, Green Digital Finance Alliance

The Fintech Job report is a timely and insightful report . Fintech is part of re-designing our labour markets through accelerating the demand for digital skills and literacy, not to say everyone should become a software developer but rather that computational thinking, digital user experience design and re-structuring of processes with data are skills of today and tomorrow. Diving into the Fintech Job report offers a great way to get access to the newest trends and analytic insights.

Matteo Rizzi
Published Author, FinTech Investor and Entrepreneur

I love the work Tram Ahn and Huy are doing to foster financial wealth, and their drive towards emerging markets. Talent development, entrepreneurial culture, and jump starting skills can bring a your entrepreneur a long way. Let's learn from the first decade of FinTech and make the next ten years more fair, sustainable and inclusive as it should.

Monica Jasuja
Fintech and Payments Product Executive

Fintech headlines have captured the world stage especially after COVID (VC investing, blockbuster IPOs, minted unicorns) creating a frenzy among job seekers. The Fintech Job Report is a boon for everyone to equip themselves to participate and capitalize from CFTE's research & invaluable insights. A real knowledge treasure trove.

Musheer Ahmed
Founder, FinStep Asia

Fintech is becoming embedded in every aspect of our lives and there is increasing competition for top talent to enable it. This report by CFTE is another excellent resource for both companies and job seekers alike to not only benchmark, but to also plan for what lies ahead in the coming future.

Foreword

Nick Ogden
Fintech Entrepreneur

Hiring the right team is vital for every Fintech start-up and scale-up business. Whilst historic candidate work experience may initially help, the ability to see over the hedge and a desire to create and embrace change is vital to these innovative businesses. These skills are hard to find, and near impossible to train, so good hiring is key. The Fintech job report is an important and overdue industry initiative.
Well done CFTE.

Dr. Oriol Caudevilla
Co-Leader of the Financial Inclusion and CBDC Working Groups at the Global Impact FinTech (GIFT) Forum

This Report, which is the first ever-made in-depth analysis on the FinTech labour market, fills a much needed gap, since the pandemic has turbocharged a financial technology (FinTech) revolution worldwide, to the point that many job seekers are looking for jobs in the FinTech industry rather than the traditional financial sector.

Paolo Sironi
Global Research Leader for Banking and Financial Markets, IBM Consulting

New ideas are found at the intersections between industries, cultures, and competencies. All professions are being transformed at the crossroads between digital and finance. Opening our personal mindset and educational journey to unconventional ideas and experiences is what it takes to master the fast overlapping between technology and business.

Dr. Paramsothy Vijayan
Director, ABS Centre of Excellence in Digital Banking

As the way we live, bank and work continues to change dramatically, we must address the magnitude of the disruptions before us. We are prepared to radically transform the way we work by introducing a comprehensive range of measures which include implementing a permanent hybrid work model, flexible work arrangements and deploying more agile squads while creating workspaces that will help to supercharge ideation and collaboration. We will also accelerate our employee upskilling agenda at scale and ingrain the use of data-driven operating models across the bank. By implementing these measures, we believe that Team DBS will emerge as a confident future-ready workforce.

Foreword

Philippe Gelis
CEO at Kantox

Finance is eventually the biggest industry ever to be disrupted by technology and new business models. The last decade was about transparency, lower prices, and better user experience. It is now time to build fundamentally new products and to create new categories.

Ritesh Jain
Founder - Infynit, Former COO Digital - HSBC

Every business will have a role to play in the Fintech ecosystems. Fintechs are working as a catalyst to unleash and unlock the potential of incumbents. With the exponential growth and recent investments, Fintechs require a skilled workforce. CFTEs guide focuses on the fintech sector, in-depth view on skills and jobs in fintech, one of the best guides in the Fintech from Fintech experts.

Ronit Ghose
Global Head, Banking, Fintech & Digital Assets - Citi Global Insights

FinTech is eating the world. Most financial services have been provided by companies built in the Industrial Revolution not the Internet Age. As we race to the next generation of the digital world, financial services is being reshaped. And with it, so are jobs. As this study explores: Fintech jobs are growing, while TradFi jobs are shrinking, "tech" jobs predominate in FinTech, but soft skills, a growth mindset and business understanding are also key.

Shameek Kundu
Head of Financial Services, TruEra Inc.

The world of Fintech can be both exciting and confusing. What does it take to work and thrive in this rapidly evolving space? Huy and Tram Anh have a unique perspective on the Fintech skills agenda, and this timely report from them is a fantastic place to start.

The Fintech Job Report: Technology is eating finance

Foreword

Sophie Guibaud
Co-founder & Chief Commercial and Growth Officer at Fiat Republic

A very comprehensive review and outlook of existing jobs in the Fintech industry and on the essential skills of the future to strive in it. In an embedded finance era, this is a must read.

Stephan Murer
Owner of Murer Consulting GmbH

Mastering information technology has always been a key driver to success in the finance industry. However, the classical banking industry with its culture and its management practices increasingly struggles to attract technology talent. Bringing technology culture to the financial industry, Fintech may bridge this gap.

Theodora Lau
Founder of Unconventional Ventures and Co-Author of Beyond Good

Technology is an integral part of everything that we do, including financial services. Financial technology, or fintech, has undergone tremendous growth. In "Technology is eating finance", CFTE takes us through the transformation of fintech and what it takes to become part of this growing ecosystem. Hop on — this is a ride that you wouldn't want to miss.

Xavier Gomez
Founder of INVYO

CFTE's initiative is part of a world in full transition that is seeing its models, values and economy greatly change. Financial education is no exception. Finance has become more democratic with the digital transformation through the advent of Fintech solutions. This is why expertise remains one of the only assets that professionals must cultivate throughout their careers to remain efficient. This book will help guide financiers in the new professions that are emerging in Finance

Executive Summary

With an ever-increasing global adoption rate, the Fintech industry has become a large source of employment opportunities, thus representing a viable option for professionals and students, whether they have a background in financial services, tech, or other industries.

The Fintech Job Report aims to provide an overview of the jobs offered by Fintech companies, analyse the skills required to join this new sector and discuss the consequences for individuals and the ramifications for the industry.

More broadly, since digital finance is rapidly growing, new roles are being created whereas others are becoming obsolete. This requires a renewed awareness of opportunities borne out of Fintech growth for job seekers, hiring organisations, governments, regulators, and higher education institutes.

Since Fintech is a fast developing industry, finding and analysing relevant and up to date data will always prove a challenge. However, the analysis of quantitative and qualitative data combined with CFTE's knowledge of the industry, should give readers a good understanding of the **trends** in Fintech jobs today.

After the research was conducted, we decided to title the report **"Technology is eating finance"**. This is because at their core, Fintech companies are Tech companies rather than financial institutions. Other key findings of the report include:

- **Significant amount of money has been invested in Fintech**. In the last decade, more than $200bn has been invested by Venture Capital and Private Equity in Fintech startups.

- **Fintech has become a major part of financial services.** The Fintech sector is now equivalent to 38% of the banking sector in terms of market capitalisation.

- **The Fintech industry is an important employer.** If Fintech was a city, it would rank third as an employer in financial services, just after New York and London. The Fintech industry currently employs 300,000 people (450,000 for New York, and 400,000 London)

Executive Summary

- **Fintech companies are aggressively hiring.** The main Fintech companies are looking to hire 40,000 professionals.

- **Fintech jobs are not standardised yet.** Fintech jobs are offered by young and fast growing companies, which create their organisation and job structures as they grow. Job titles, requirements and responsibilities therefore tend to differ between organisations.

- **There are 14 main job families in Fintech.** Despite the lack of standardisation, the report identifies 14 main job families, such as Engineering or Product Development.

- **Job families can be categorised as "Generic", "Tech" or "Finance".** As an industry that brings together technology and finance, most jobs fall into one of these 3 categories: 1) Jobs usually found in Tech companies. 2) Jobs usually found in financial services. 3) Jobs found in all companies

- **"Tech" jobs are predominant in Fintech.** 70 to 90% of the non-generic jobs in Fintech are jobs that would normally be found in Tech firms. Finance jobs are much less frequent in Fintech.

- **Hard skills are important, but not sufficient.** Hard skills such as programming or data science might be the first things that come to mind when thinking about Fintech, but there are many other requirements of hard skills depending on the job roles. Interestingly, Mindset, Soft Skills and Industry Knowledge, are equally important for Fintech companies, but usually overlooked by applicants.

- **Transferable skills to get into Fintech are more "Tech" than "Fin".** Although an understanding of finance is helpful in Fintech, this is not the main requirement for Fintech companies. Digital skills, Fintech understanding and an entrepreneur mindset tend to be more sought after skills by recruiters.

- **Fintech and traditional finance jobs are likely to converge.** Although Fintech jobs are today quite different from traditional finance, the convergence of both into digital finance is likely to lead to a convergence of job roles too. The major difference between roles in both types of organisations is the culture and mindset of employees, and it is to be seen if there will be convergence in that area too.

Introduction

Since the subprime crisis of 2008, the financial industry has been profoundly reshaped by the Fintech phenomenon, i.e. the accelerated use of technology in financial services. The most notable impact was the rise of new entrants, especially Fintech startups, which surfed on the wave of new consumer behaviours, adoption of mobile technologies and regulatory changes.

While Fintech was a confidential sector a decade ago, it has now grown to be an important part of financial services. Consumers have widely adopted Fintech, with an adoption rate of 64% globally and 96% of consumers aware of at least one Fintech service (Global Fintech Adoption Index 2019, EY).This in turn led to the market capitalisation of the largest Fintech companies now equalling to almost 40% of the largest banks. Record amounts of money are being invested and the industry is growing at an exponential rate.

To support this business growth, Fintech companies have significantly grown their workforce. The sector now employs more than 300,000 people and is hiring more than 40,000 professionals, making it almost the size of leading financial centres such as London or New York, however, Fintech is hiring 3 or 4 times faster.

While a job in Fintech was not an obvious option for most professionals and students a few years ago, it is now clearly an alternative to be considered: salaries are high and career opportunities are flourishing thanks to the overall industry growth.

If Fintech is an attractive sector, what are the ways to get in? Because of the "**Fin**" in **Fin**tech, it might seem natural that professionals with a background in financial services have the best transferable skills for Fintech, after all, many Fintech startups were started by founders with an experience in finance. The reality today is however different. The "**Tech**" in Fin**tech** is the most predominant for Fintech jobs, and Fintech companies are much closer to Tech than finance companies. This is why this report is titled **"Tech is eating finance"**.

Introduction

For those interested in a job in finance and Fintech, this report should serve as a good starting point to understand the jobs available, and the skills required by Fintech companies - including the importance of not just hard skills, but perhaps even more mindset, soft skills and industry knowledge.

More generally, this report also raises important questions for the industry at large. While the Fintech industry is a significant employer, very few students are prepared for, or even aware of these opportunities. This should therefore be an area of focus for the higher education system.

Furthermore, as finance becomes a digital industry, there is little doubt that many jobs in financial services will be converging towards Fintech jobs. This should be a priority for banks and insurers to reflect upon.

And finally, as Fintech is becoming a large part of FS, but is at its core (i.e. its people) a Tech industry, there will be implications for governments and regulators to think about, such as competitiveness, talent development or supervision.

This first edition of the Fintech Job Report is being written at a time when Fintech is already starting to make a large impact in financial services, which has been accelerated even further due to COVID-19. This means that as an industry, Fintech is likely to continue developing rapidly, and evolve into a dominant employer on the global job market. There will be important opportunities for many, and we hope that this report is a starting point to understand what these are.

Part 1
The Growth of Fintech Startups

The Fintech Job Report

Although the finance industry has always been a significant user of technology, the "Fintech" phenomenon as we know it now really started after the 2008 subprime crisis, where the convergence between changing **consumer behaviour**, **mobile technology** and **regulations** facilitated the rise of new players in financial services.

This is when innovations started such as **peer-to-peer lending, crowdfunding, Bitcoin, Blockchain, data-driven lending**, pioneered by the nascent Fintech ecosystem.

Since then, the industry has profoundly matured and has grown tremendously, both in terms of its size and impact.

This was supported by an accelerating inflow of venture money - which started at around $3bn / year 10 years ago, to an average of $50bn every year now. Overall, more than $200bn has been invested in Fintech startups globally. Although this is a very large amount, this is to be considered within the context of financial services, which is a very large industry and where operating expenses of JP Morgan Chase amount to $100bn annually.

FIGURE 1

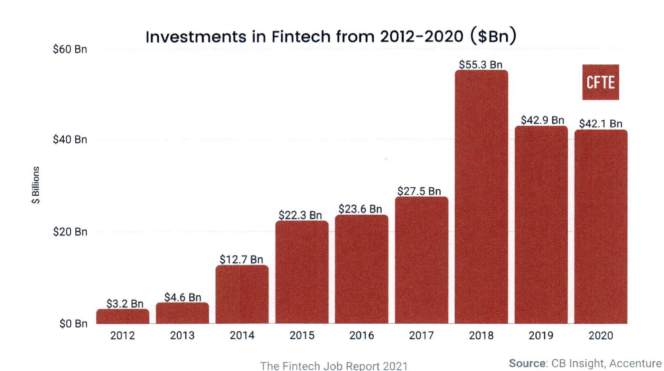

Source: CB Insight, Accenture

Despite the high enthusiasm of investors for Fintech startups, there were significant doubts about the potential for new entrants to break the regulated world of financial services, and where consumers rank trust very highly in their relationship with their financial providers. These doubts were unfounded, however, and consumers quickly used Fintech, with global adoption raising from 16% in 2015 to 64% in 2019 (Global Fintech Adoption Index 2019, EY).

FIGURE 2

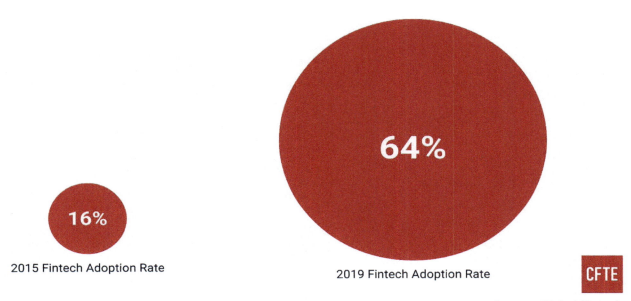

User adoption helped the growth of Fintech startups, which have now grown both in quantity and in size. Overall, there are now 225 Fintech "Unicorns", i.e. companies which are valued at more than $1bn. Although valuations are always a tricky number to represent the impact of companies, this is however a helpful reminder that the Fintech industry has hugely evolved, from tiny startups to billion-dollar international companies.

The Growth of Fintech Startups

The 225 Fintech Unicorns and their Valuation

Company	Valuation	Company	Valuation	Company	Valuation	Company	Valuation
Visa	$490B	Du Xiaoman Financial	$4B	Unqork	$2B	Public	$1B
Mastercard	$350B	Melio	$4B	Tipalti	$2B	DailyPay	$1B
Ant Financial	$312B	Kraken	$4B	Ethos Technologies	$2B	CoinDCX	$1B
Paypal	$306B	Wealthsimple	$4B	Clip	$2B	Zego	$1B
Tencent (Fintech business)	$120B	Next Insurance	$4B	EBANX	$2B	Sunbit	$1B
Square	$110B	iCapital Network	$4B	Digit Insurance	$2B	Radius Payment Solutions	$1B
Stripe	$95B	Airwallex	$4B	CoinSwitch	$2B	Flutterwave	$1B
Adyen	$84B	FalconX	$4B	Starling Bank	$2B	Interswitch	$1B
Coinbase	$52B	Papaya Global	$4B	MX Technologies	$2B	Chipper Cash	$1B
Aspire	$40B	N26	$4B	Judo Bank	$2B	Riskified	$1B
Affirm	$38B	Payoneer	$3B	SpotOn	$2B	WeLab	$1B
Robinhood	$36B	Blend	$3B	CFGI	$2B	Liquid Global	$1B
Gojek	$35B	Figure Technologies	$3B	Fawry	$2B	Earnix	$1B
Revolut	$33B	Cedar	$3B	Trulioo	$2B	Amber Group	$1B
Klarna	$31B	Blockstream	$3B	Creditas	$2B	VNLife	$1B
Nubank	$30B	Lakala	$3B	Wave	$2B	Nium	$1B
Bill.com	$27B	HighRadius	$3B	Pleo	$2B	Matrixport	$1B
UIPath	$26B	Razorpay	$3B	Alan	$2B	Xendit	$1B
Paytm	$25B	Pine Labs	$3B	solarisBank	$2B	JimuBox	$1B
Chime	$25B	Groww	$3B	Bunq	$2B	Liquid	$1B
Upstart	$24B	Wefox	$3B	Ramp	$2B	Dunamu	$1B
Tinkoff	$20B	BGL Group	$3B	Extend	$2B	Bolttech	$1B
Ally Financial	$19B	Circle	$3B	Mercury	$2B	Vendantu	$1B
FTX	$18B	Blockfi	$3B	Opay	$2B	Ajaib	$1B
Marqeta	$16B	Upgrade	$3B	Hyperchain	$2B	Shift Technology	$1B
Xero	$15B	Ovo	$3B	Betternet	$2B	Honeybook	$1B
Checkout.com	$15B	BharatPe	$3B	Qudian	$2B	PPRO	$1B
Wise	$15B	Drivewealth	$3B	Fundbox	$2B	Numbrs	$1B
Grab	$14B	Oaknorth	$3B	Remitly	$2B	Raisin	$1B
Plaid	$14B	Paidy	$3B	Ledger	$2B	Lunar	$1B
Sofi	$13B	Tradeshift	$3B	Enfusion	$2B	Tractable	$1B
StoneCo	$10B	Toss	$3B	Collective Health	$2B	SumUp	$1B
Ripple	$10B	Read Morelogis	$3B	Persona	$2B	SaltPay	$1B
Gusto	$10B	Divvy	$3B	Guideline	$2B	TrueLayer	$1B
Oscar Health	$10B	Ualá	$2B	Built	$2B	SmartAsset	$1B
Rapyd	$9B	Policybazaar	$2B	Zeta	$1B	Dave	$1B
Lufax	$9B	cgtz	$2B	ChargeBee Technologies	$1B	Varo Money	$1B
Toast	$8B	Paxos	$2B	Scalable Capital	$1B	WeBull	$1B
Brex	$8B	Greenlight	$2B	Symphony	$1B	Vise	$1B
Better.com	$8B	C6 Bank	$2B	M1 Finance	$1B	Trumid	$1B
Dapper Labs	$8B	Cred	$2B	Stash	$1B	Tresata	$1B
Viva Republica	$7B	Izettle	$2B	At-Bay	$1B	Sidecar Health	$1B
Lemonade	$7B	Acorns	$2B	Alloy	$1B	Pacaso	$1B
Carta	$7B	Current	$2B	Signifyd	$1B	Ivalua	$1B
Mollie	$7B	Fireblocks	$2B	TaxBit	$1B	Ibotta	$1B
Avant	$7B	Bitso	$2B	Enova	$1B	Forte Labs	$1B
True Accord	$6B	Addepar	$2B	Feedzai	$1B	Clearcover	$1B
Zhong An	$6B	Tink	$2B	Ascend Money	$1B	Amount	$1B
Trade Republic	$5B	Green Sky	$2B	Socure	$1B	Qualia	$1B
Blockchain.com	$5B	ReCharge	$2B	Konfio	$1B	Injective Protocol	$1B
Flywire	$5B	Mercado Bitcoin	$2B	Root Insurance	$1B	MobileCoin	$1B
QuintoAndar	$5B	Waterdrop	$2B	BlockDaemon	$1B	Orchard	$1B
WorldRemit	$5B	Mambu	$2B	Monzo	$1B	Sightline Payments	$1B
Hippo Insurance	$5B	Bought By Many	$2B	Marshmallow	$1B	FreshBooks	$1B
Sorare	$4B	AvidXchange	$2B	Deel	$1B		
Chainalysis	$4B	Clearbanc	$2B	Bitpanda	$1B		
Dataminr	$4B	Pipe	$2B	Kabbage	$1B		

If we were to compare Fintech startups to the traditional financial institutions, 10 years ago, the whole Fintech industry represented almost nothing compared to banking - less than 3%.

Today, this is not the case. The 100 largest banks have a combined market capitalisation of $7.1 trillion, while the 100 largest Fintech companies have a combined market capitalisation of $2.8 trillion. In other words, Fintech as an industry is as big as 38% of banking. These are incredible numbers considering that Fintech has been around for 10 years vs. hundreds of years for banking.

FIGURE 3

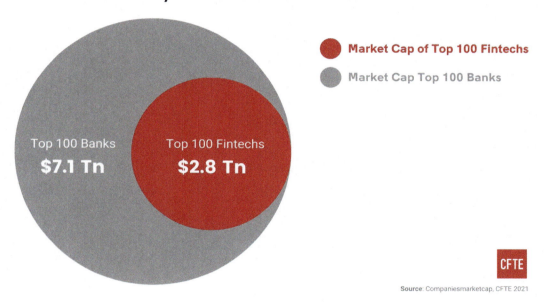

However, we would not want to give the impression that "Fintech = Growth" vs. "Bank = Decline". At CFTE, our definition of Fintech is "the impact of technology in financial services", and this includes not only Fintech startups, but also banks and tech companies. This distinction between Fintech startups and traditional finance is likely to be more and more blurry in the future as these worlds converge.

Most of these companies are private companies, usually funded by Venture Capital and Private Equity, and less than 10% are public companies.

FIGURE 4

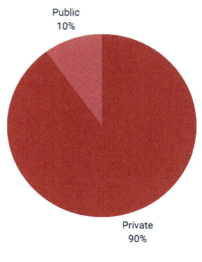

In terms of geographical distribution, the US is the undisputed leader for Fintech companies, both in terms of the number of companies and overall amount. It is then followed by the UK and China and India, although China is a clear second in terms of market valuations thanks to Ant Group and Tencent.

FIGURE 5

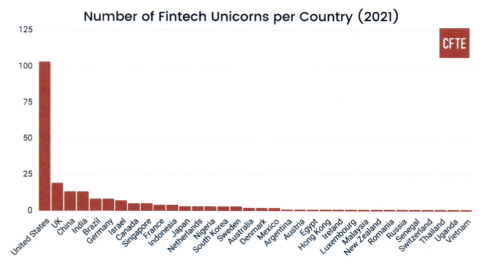

The Growth of Fintech Startups

And finally, these companies are present in the whole spectrum of financial services - including new sectors such as cryptocurrencies and Blockchain. The most frequent sectors are Payments, Challenger Banks, Wealthtech, Infrastructure and Insurtech.

FIGURE 6

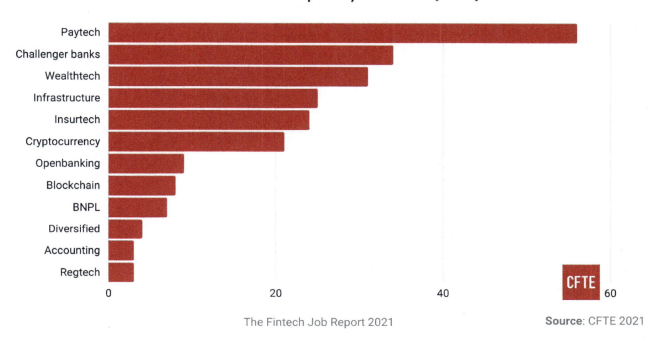

The Fintech Job Report 2021 — Source: CFTE 2021

Part 2
Fintech as an Employer

The Fintech Job Report

As the Fintech industry has grown, it has also led to more employment opportunities. Whereas a decade ago, Fintech was mainly attracting those interested to join small unproven startups, this is now a much more mature industry, both in terms of size and stability of jobs offered.

Our analysis of the 225 Fintech companies shows that they employ **300,000** people. This ranges from more than 25,000 people for Paypal down to 200 for the smallest organisations.

On average, each of these Fintech companies employs 1,300 people, which in itself is a relatively small number compared to financial institutions that employ tens or hundreds of thousands.

FIGURE 7

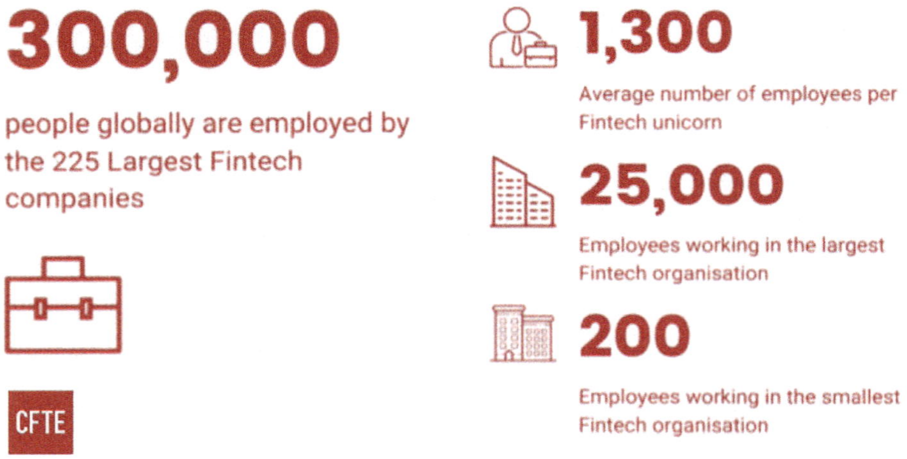

300,000

people globally are employed by the 225 Largest Fintech companies

1,300
Average number of employees per Fintech unicorn

25,000
Employees working in the largest Fintech organisation

200
Employees working in the smallest Fintech organisation

As an industry, Fintech has reached a reasonable size as an employer. For example, New York as a financial centre employs 450,000 people. London, 400,000. Which would make Fintech at 300,000 people the 3rd largest city, just behind New York and London. Considering that Fintech jobs also tend to be highly qualified, well paid jobs, this comparison with world-leading financial centres describes well the importance of Fintech as an employer.

FIGURE 8   Fintech as an Employer

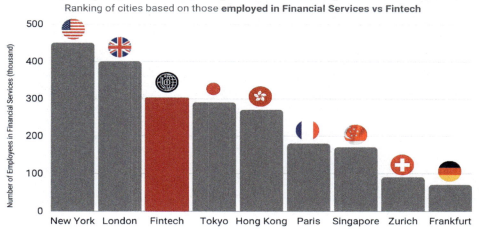

In October 2021, there were 40,000 open positions in the 225 Fintech companies, i.e. an average of 180 jobs per company. As a comparison, the finance industry was advertising for 10,000 jobs in London during the same period.

FIGURE 9

40,000
open positions in Fintech

10,000
open positions in London
(Financial Services)

The number of open positions is high, but underestimates the growth of the Fintech sector. These numbers only reflect the jobs offered at a certain time, but as these jobs are filled up and new hiring needs arise, the number of open positions will fluctuate. Although it is difficult to have an exact number, we estimate that the Fintech industry might advertise between 80,000 to 100,000 jobs in the next year.

To summarise, the Fintech industry is now a large employer, on par with large financial centres such as London or Tokyo, and offers similar levels of salaries. In addition, it is growing much faster than traditional finance, and can therefore represent an interesting sector for professionals and students alike.

Part 3
The Jobs in Fintech

The Fintech Job Report

With 300,000 people employed in Fintech, and 40,000 jobs offered by the largest Fintech companies, there is no shortage of information about job descriptions and job roles for Fintech. However, making sense of this information is a challenging task because of a **lack of taxonomy** for Fintech jobs.

Since traditional finance is an industry that has matured over a long period of time, there is a good understanding of the job families and job roles in its various sectors. For example, Singapore's Institute of Banking and Finance has a comprehensive map of roles for retail banking, corporate banking, investment banking, asset management, private banking and insurance, across functions such as sales, trading or operations (The Skills Framework for Financial Services, IBF) These details provide candidates with the job description, generic skills & competencies with their proficiency level required for each role and outlines the career trajectory for various roles and sectors.

In the Fintech space, creating this taxonomy is more challenging because this is a new and fast growing sector, and where companies employ hundreds or thousands of people, i.e. 100 times less than the large financial institutions. So whereas a bank might have 100 people in one specific function, a Fintech company might have just one, and a purely quantitative analysis of job roles is less relevant.

In addition, Fintech companies create jobs and roles on a need basis. Companies might therefore have very different requirements for roles which are similarly named. For example, a Product Manager at Lemonade might be expected to have very strong domain expertise (in that case insurance), whereas a Product Manager at Square might be required to be much more technical and API-driven.

With this in mind, categorising jobs in Fintech today faces the following challenges:
- As Fintech companies grow, they create positions that are specific to their circumstances and might not be suited to other organisations
- Some jobs did not exist a few years ago
- Fintech companies might create a job title that has little equivalence
- A role with the same job title might mean something totally different between two organisations
- Fintech is a broad industry that includes sectors as diverse as insurance and cryptocurrencies, with very different job requirements

Challenges to Categorise Fintech Jobs

Jobs that did not exist
Jobs specific to each company
Different job titles
Same job titles but different jobs
Very broad sector

Because of these constraints, a taxonomy of Fintech jobs is likely to remain quite fluid until the industry becomes much more mature, although it is certainly much more advanced than a few years ago.

The approach taken by the Fintech Job Report is to combine quantitative and qualitative analysis together with expert insights to create an overview of the Fintech jobs that can be directly useful to the industry.

14 Main Fintech Job Families

The analysis finds that there are 14 main job families most commonly found across the 40,000 jobs advertised.

The 14 job families are:

- Business Development,
- Core Business,
- Customer Support,
- Data Science,
- Design,
- Engineering,
- Finance,
- Human Resources,
- IT & Operations,
- Legal,
- Marketing & Communications,
- Partnerships,
- Product Management,
- Risk & Compliance.

In the same way that organisations change their organisation chart and structure on a regular basis, there are unlimited options to categorise the job families in Fintech. Some Fintech companies might have Partnerships as part of Business Development. Data Science could be merged with Engineering, or Design could be part of Product. Our research hasn't found any standardised structure for Fintech companies, and this categorisation in 14 job families should be a good starting point for most organisations.

3 Main Types of Job Families

The 14 job families could be grouped in different ways, either through similarities (for example Business Development and Marketing) or frequency of jobs offered.

Taking the perspective of applicants, and also Fintech entrepreneurs, we decided to group the job families according to the **type of organisations**. Based on this approach, we found that Fintech job families fall into 3 categories: jobs found in most organisations, Jobs found in Tech companies, jobs found in financial services.

Jobs Found in Most Organisations

4 job families are included in this category:
- Legal
- Human Resources
- Finance Department
- Customer Service

Although these jobs are extremely important for the growth of Fintech companies, they are not necessarily different from other organisations and will not be analysed in this report.

Jobs Found in Tech Companies

8 job families are included in this category:
- Engineering
- Data Science
- IT & Operations
- Product Management
- Design
- Business Development
- Partnership
- Marketing & Communication

Going deeper, these job families can be divided into 2 further groups:
- Tech jobs, i.e. mainly technical jobs
- Non-tech, or business jobs

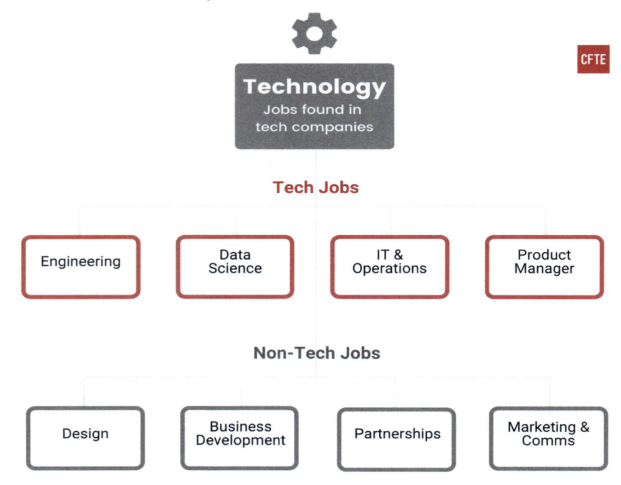

Jobs found in financial services

2 job families are included in this category:
- Risk & Compliance
- Core business

Core business means activities that are directly related to the core business of the Fintech company. For example, a Challenger Bank that offers lending would have a treasury function. Or an Insurtech would have underwriters to price their policies. Core business will be therefore different for Fintechs operating in different sectors.

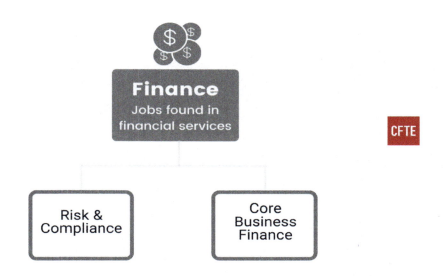

14 Job Families in 3 Main Categories

Overall, the jobs in Fintech can be grouped into 14 main job families that would normally be found in 1) most organisations, 2) Tech companies and 3) financial services.

Job families from Tech companies are the most frequent, with 8 families identified. It is then followed by the generic category with 4 families, and then financial services with 2.

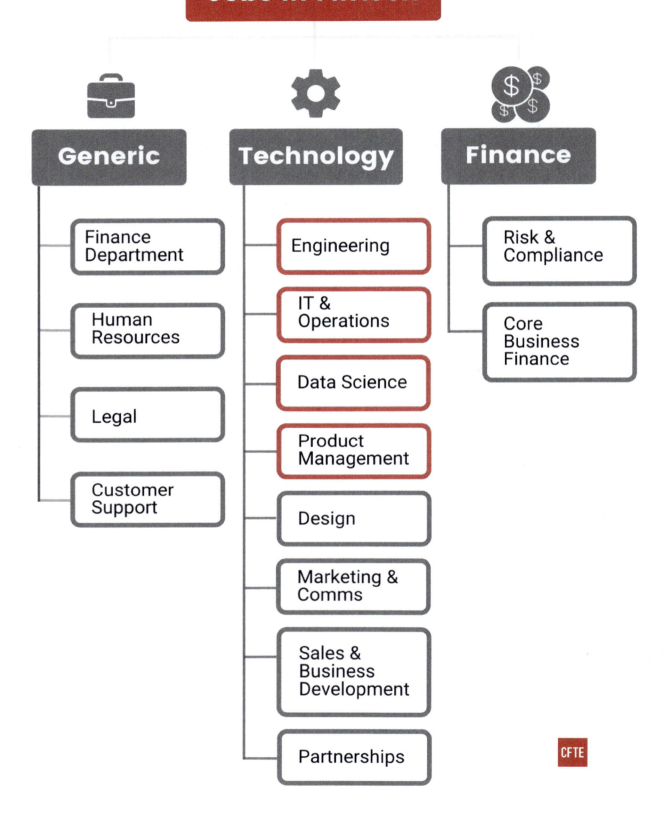

If we were to only consider the number of job families, Fintech companies would be much more similar to Tech companies than financial companies. This might be different however if some job families had much more employees than others. We therefore analysed the number of job openings per family across 9 sectors:

1. Payments

The payments sector as represented by Square and Stripe saw a large increase in jobs due to its rapid expansion during the Covid-19 pandemic and the consequent increase in cashless payments.

The sector has 37% of engineering roles. Sales & Business development with 15%, IT & Operations with 11%, Risk & Compliance with 7% respectively were the next most common roles. Additionally, Core Business Finance roles 7%, Product Management with 6%, Marketing with 7% and design with 5% follow suit on the next most common roles in the payments sector. Lastly, Partnerships with 2% and Data Science with 4% occupy the least common roles in the payments sector.

2. Challenger Banks

Fintech jobs in the Challenger Banks sector such as Nubank or Revolut have engineering 29%, product management 12% and Risk & Compliance 15% as the most common jobs. These sectors also showed opportunities in Sales & Business development 10%, Core Business Finance 9%, Data Science 7%, Design 7%, Marketing 6%, IT & Operations 5% and finally, the partnerships roles were the least common in the sector with 1% of the jobs advertised.

3. Wealthtech

Fintechs like Robinhood and Better.com were analysed with most common roles being Engineering 29%, IT & Operations 16%, Data Science 12%, Risk & Compliance 11% with lower recruitment trends being in Core Business Finance 8%, Design 8%, Product Management 7%. Additionally, these three families had less than 5% recruitment opportunities in Wealthtech: Sales and BD 4%, Marketing 3% and Partnerships 2%.

4. Lending
Another Fintech sector analysed was Lending with companies like Upstart or SoFi. The lending sector has Engineering 31%, IT & Operations 21% and Sales and BD 12%. They are followed by Product Management 9%, Core Business Finance 7%, Marketing 6% and Data Science 5%. Finally, Risk & Compliance 4%, Design 4% and Partnerships 3% have the lowest count of job roles.

5. Buy Now Pay Later
We analysed the Buy Now Pay Later sector with companies like Klarna and Affirm. These sectors highlighted most common job roles being Engineering 46%, IT & Operations 12% and Product Management 10%. Other job roles had Marketing 8% Sales and BD 6%, Core Business Finance 5% and Data Science 5% with the roles with fewer hiring numbers being Design 3%, Risk & Compliance 3% and Partnerships 1%.

6. Insurtech
Job families in the Insurtech sector like Oscar and Lemonade highlighted the most common roles being around Engineering 36%, Risk & Compliance 22% and Core Business Finance 13%. The following common roles are Data Science 8%, Product Management 6% and Marketing 6%. Additional roles with fewer job roles were Sales and BD 4%, Design 2%, Partnerships 2% and IT & Operations 1%.

7. Infrastructure
In infrastructure companies such as Plaid or Truelayer the most common roles were in Engineering 34%, followed by Sales and BD 15% and Marketing 11%. Apart from these roles, the following most common are Risk & Compliance 9%, Design 9%, Product Management 7%, Partnerships 7% and Data Science 5%. The Infrastructure sector has the least common roles in Core Business Finance 2% and IT & Operations 1%.

8. Cryptocurrencies
Cryptocurrencies sector like Bitpanda and Blockchain.com highlighted the common job roles being Engineering 33%, Product Management 17% and Core Business Finance 10%. Additionally roles like Marketing 9%, IT & Operations 8%, Design 8% and Risk & Compliance 8% followed. The sector had job families that were least common being Sales and BD 3%, Data Science 2% and Partnerships 0%.

9. Blockchain

The Blockchain sector in Fintech with companies like Chainanalysis and Ripple highlighted families with the most common roles being Engineering 54% and IT & Operations 18%. Product Management 8%, Sales and BD 7% and Marketing 6% followed. Finally, the job families with less common roles were Core Business Finance 3%, Risk & Compliance 2%, Design 2%, Data Science 0% and Partnerships 0%.

FIGURE 10

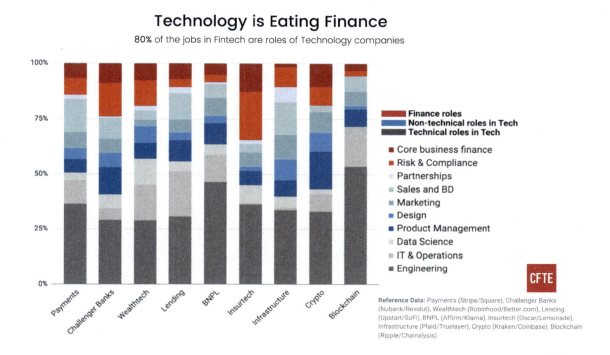

The analysis revealed the following findings:

- The "Tech" jobs represent from 70% to 90% of the job openings, with 50% to 65% being Tech roles, and the rest being non-tech
- The "Finance" jobs represent from 10 to 30% of the job openings

On average, 80% of the jobs in Fintech companies would be similar to jobs of Tech companies, which is the reason why we came up with the conclusion **"Tech is eating finance"**.

60 Job Roles in Fintech

Engineering	1. Front End Engineer 2. Backend Engineer 3. Full Stack Engineer 4. Platform Engineer 5. Machine Learning Engineer 6. Solutions Engineer 7. Data Engineer 8. Security Engineer
IT & Operations	1. Consumer Operations 2. Insurance Operations 3. Fraud Operations 4. Business Operations 5. Operational Risk
Data Science	1. Data Analyst 2. Data Engineer 3. Data Quality Analyst 4. Big Data Engineer 5. Data Scientist 6. Analytics Manager 7. Data Automation Developer 8. Business Intelligence Analyst 9. Data Infrastructure Analyst
Product Management	1. Core Business 2. Platform 3. Risk & Compliance 4. Data
Design	1. Product Designer 2. Content Designer 3. Art Director 4. UX Writer 5. UX Researcher
Marketing & Communications	1. Growth Marketer 2. Communications 3. Copywriter 4. CRM 5. Performance Marketing 6. Marketing Automation
Sales & Business Development	1. Enterprise Sales 2. Business Development 3. Sales Engineer 4. Partner Sales
Partnerships	1. Sales Partnerships 2. Marketing Partnerships 3. Marketing Partnerships
Risk & Compliance	1. Compliance Officer 2. Risk Intelligence Engineer 3. Privacy & Compliance Engineer 4. Fraud Officer 5. AML Officer 6. Financial Crime Officer 7. Cyber Fraud Investigator 8. Regulatory Policy Officer 9. Technical Program Manager
Core Business Finance	1. Credit Analyst 2. Portfolio Analyst 3. Underwriter 4. Fraud Analyst 5. Treasury Analyst 6. Claims Specialist 7. Actuary

1. Engineering

We found 8 roles in this family in charge of creating, developing, testing and maintaining software, as well as generating software ideas and communicating with necessary stakeholders to understand their requirements. These roles are very common in Fintech and Tech companies offering an easy career move from one industry to another for experienced individuals.

2. IT & Operations

There are 5 roles in this job family. These roles are important in Fintech as they form the day-to-day operations of the company including responding to user requests, monitoring and executing system backups. Additionally, these roles offer opportunities from entry level to senior positions.

3. Data Science

There are 9 roles in this job family. These roles are common in Fintech due to the large amounts of data found in the industry. These roles are important because they allow businesses to have a deep understanding of their customer base, which in turn can lead to smarter business decisions that put customer experience first. These roles have opportunities for entry level and senior level positions of 10+ years of experience.

4. Product Management

We found 4 roles in this job family. These roles are vital in Fintech due to the customer experience that the industry provides. These roles are vital in that they are in charge of overseeing the creation and development of Fintech services, as well as responsible for the whole lifecycle and the long-term strategy of the product. The opportunities in this job family are rare for the entry level positions.

5. Design

There are 5 roles in this family. The roles in this family are vital in Fintech operations galvanising the visual aspect of Fintech services and its marketing materials can have an enormous impact on customer perception and in turn acquisition. The opportunities in these roles are influenced by nature and seniority but entry level positions are available.

6. Marketing & Communications
There are 5 roles in this family. Marketing and Communications and important in Fintech as they offer effective engagement with potential and existing customers for companies. Job opportunities in these roles are available for entry level positions to senior level positions with a keen interest in practical knowledge.

7. Sales & Business Development
There are 4 roles in this family. These roles are vital for niche markets for day-to-day operations. Practical knowledge of these responsibilities award opportunities for both entry level and senior level positions in Fintech.

8. Partnerships
There are 3 roles in this family. These are important roles in charge of customer acquisition and service delivery. Due to the relatively new introduction of this role into Fintech, it is available commonly for senior positions.

9. Risk & Compliance
There are 9 roles in this family. The risk & compliance roles are common and vital in Fintech due to the regulatory and risk management nuances in the Fintech industry. These roles are mostly mid-level to senior level positions with rare entry level positions of less than 5 years professional experience being available.

10. Core Business Finance
There are 7 roles in this family. These roles are niche roles depending on the sector a Fintech company operates in thus having a vital role in company operations. There are entry level positions available with at least 2 years experience but commonly, senior positions are more in demand.

Conclusion
Despite the name "Fintech", the job roles in Fintech companies are quite different from traditional financial services, and much more similar to technology companies. Excluding the generic roles, 8 out of 10 job families are found in Tech companies, and 2 out of 10 are found in financial services. A good understanding of Tech companies is therefore helpful to understand how Fintech companies function, at least in terms of roles and organisation. It does not mean however that there are no specific requirements due to the nature of the Fintech activity, and this is analysed in the next chapter where skills are discussed.

Part 4
The Skills in Fintech

The Fintech Job Report

As seen from the growth of Fintech, the evolution of Fintech roles is still ongoing, meaning that while some new roles are being created, others are becoming obsolete. A need arises for candidates, recruiters and learning institutions to understand the skills needed for the roles discussed in the previous chapter.

A good understanding of the required skills is important for the candidates who want to apply, but also those who want to upskill or reskill to be relevant for a world of digital finance. It is also critical for recruiters to identify the critical skills for their organisations. Additionally, learning institutions, regulators and governments can benefit from aligning their training programmes to skills most in demand in the industry. This in turn ensures that the industry finds the right talents, which then fuels its growth. The Fintech industry has a wide range of job roles, our research determined the skills needed for these roles are hard skills, soft skills, mindset, industry knowledge and experience.

The Skills of Fintech

Hard Skills

Soft Skills

Mindset

Industry Knowledge

Experience

In our analysis, we differentiated the skills in the following ways:

- **Hard skills**: skills which are measurable, for example in the form of an assessment, multiple choice questions, or project. *For example Python or Open Banking regulations.*
- **Soft skills**: "human" traits which can be less easily measured. *For example collaboration or leadership.*
- **Mindset**: way of thinking, that is reflected in one's behaviour. *For example adaptability or resilience.*
- **Industry knowledge**: industry, sector, or general knowledge. *For example applications of AI in compliance or Fintech ecosystem.*
- **Experience**: either work or degree. *For example experience in e-commerce of BSc in Computer Science.*

Hard Skills

Hard skills are those that can be examined and assessed through an exam or project such as a programming language e.g. Python or open banking regulations. Most emphasis is placed on acquiring and showing know-how in hard skills. Since Fintech roles are closer to those in Tech roles, roles such as engineering and data science may come to mind, however, as mentioned previously there are non-tech roles that fall under this category showcasing the opportunities in Fintech with the right skills which contrast with programming such as a product manager applying design thinking, and a compliance officer experienced in Anti Money Laundering regulations.

The Hard Skills Required in Fintech

Engineering	➢ JavaScript, Python, Ruby, PHP HTML and CSS ➢ Node.js ➢ Databases and infrastructures ➢ Cloud platforms (AWS, GCP…) ➢ APIs
IT & Operations	➢ Network administration ➢ Device administration ➢ Service operations ➢ Experience in SQL, Python, Excel
Data Science	➢ Database operations ➢ Data visualisation tools (Tableau, Power BI…) ➢ Programming languages (R, Python, SQL) ➢ Cloud platforms (AWS, GCP…) ➢ Statistics
Product Management	➢ Product analytics ➢ Product testing methodologies ➢ Customer research methodologies ➢ Data analytics and data science for Risk and Compliance and Data

Design	➢ Digital designing tools (Sketch, Figma, Adobe Photoshop, InVision, Canva Pro…) ➢ Creating and editing videos ➢ Photography ➢ Typography ➢ Microsoft Office Suite ➢ UX/UI
Marketing & Communications	➢ Writing and copywriting skills ➢ Ability to write and create for multiple channels ➢ Marketing automation ➢ Web analytics ➢ Adobe Creative Suite ➢ Microsoft Suite
Sales & Business Development	➢ Technical skills for software such as CRM, Collaboration software ➢ Sales and marketing
Partnerships	➢ Project/product management ➢ Experience in technology and industry ➢ Software such as salesforce
Risk & Compliance	➢ AML legislation + regulation ➢ Database operations ➢ Finance operations
Core Business Finance	➢ Microsoft Office Suite (especially Excel and Powerpoint) ➢ Data Analysis ➢ Financial Modelling and Analysis ➢ Statistics and Mathematics ➢ R, Python, SQL ➢ Theoretical knowledge of finance

Soft Skills

Soft skills are less tangible and measurable in contrast with hard skills. These are human qualities that relate to a candidate's interactions with colleagues, customers and overall management of work. While the general perception is that hard skills are important, soft skills influence the success and progression of a career in Fintech. Learning institutions may supplement their learning with soft skills and those working may develop soft skills from these experiences but ultimately an individual's proactivity determines their application of these soft skills and overall value addition to the team and company they work in.

Soft skills across the roles were similar and most popular include: communication, presentation skills and collaboration both internally and externally. These skills enable smooth processes and delivery of work especially for roles involved in cross-functional teamwork as the language and relationships with different stakeholders are nuanced. Other common soft skills include multi-tasking, time management and project management, which are important in the oversight of different tasks one may need in Fintech with the result being effective and seamless delivery of service to the consumers. Additionally, interpersonal skills, negotiation skills, active listening skills, customer service, and stakeholder management are key in driving engagement in Fintech, an important aspect in both customer service, funding and partnerships, and overall teamwork in a company.

The Soft Skills Required in Fintech

Collaboration	Communication
Listening Skills	Attention to Details
Time Management	Presentation Skills
Multitasking	Organisational Skills
Stakeholder Management	Project Management
Negotiation	Interpersonal Skills

Mindset

Hard skills and Soft skills cover a large area of the requirements in getting into the Fintech industry but mindset ensures longevity and success of a career, better teamwork, individual work ethic, and the possibility of a company to succeed in its objective. Mindset is a way of thinking that is reflected in one's behaviour, for example, adaptability or resilience. Fintech has grown exponentially from startups to large organisations, and **thinking like an entrepreneur** is the best way to summarise the mindset of Fintech. Such a mindset includes; adaptability, resilience, being comfortable with uncertainty, problem-solving, and willingness to learn. These mindsets allow individuals to innovate, upskill/reskill and grow in the Fintech industry. Mindsets do not vary much on specific roles but some like having a learner mindset and adaptability are crucial to anyone working in the industry.

The Mindset Required in Fintech

Entrepreneurial Mindset	Ability to Deal with Ambiguity
Adaptability	Continuous Learning
Proactive	Takes Ownership
Innovative	Creativity and Curiosity
Forward Thinker	Customer Oriented
Problem Solver	Empathy

Industry Knowledge

Another skill that may influence the success and introduction into Fintech careers is having industry knowledge required in Fintech. Industry knowledge is industry, sector, or general knowledge for example applications of AI in compliance or Fintech ecosystem which varies in the Fintech sector, such as open banking, finance, insurance, wealth management, etc. Industry knowledge is advantageous in getting job roles and grasping the scope of work. Fintechs hires more on experience, with entry-level jobs and internships being a rarity.

Industry knowledge is required more for people with less technical skills than technical skills citing the need for those interested in Fintech to have an understanding and clarity on the nuances of the sector they wish to join as a start. The nuances in the Fintech industry require specific knowledge on the topic from a stakeholder's perspective, enabling improved revenues for the company, increased chances for career progression, and effective policies for regulators. Individuals gain industry knowledge by networking, research, reading and industry publications to get relevant and timely information for the sector a candidate is interested in joining.

The Industry Knowledge of Fintech

Fintech Ecosystem

Trends in the Industry

Main players in Fintech

Regulations

Application of technologies to specific sectors

Experience

Finally, experience is essential for Fintech. Entry level jobs and internships are rare in Fintech, consequently making work duration and accreditations account for experience in Fintech. Fintech companies do not have high precedence over one or the other as long as a candidate proves these skills. Accreditations accepted in Fintech vary from degrees in computer science for engineering to certified anti-money laundering specialist (CAMS) certificates for compliance officers. Additionally, interest in Fintech in general, a specific sector or the company you are interested in working in, is highly advantageous in getting roles here.

Conclusion

All these skills are important to have a successful career in Fintech, no matter the role. Having soft skills such as communication and collaboration, and mindset such as **"thinking like an entrepreneur"** are strong assets for those who want to join the industry. Hard skills tend to differ based on the job roles, and can either be technical or technical depending on the position. And finally, a good understanding of the industry is always advantageous, even more in non-tech roles. In terms of experience, the Fintech industry tends to hire experienced professionals rather than young graduates, however this is likely to change as the industry matures.

Part 5
Jobs in Fintech and the Required Skills

The Fintech Job Report

Jobs in Fintech and the Required Skills

The Ideal Fintech Candidates

The Fintech Job Report

Engineering

The Ideal Fintech Candidate

HARD SKILLS

Programming languages

MINDSET

Self-learner

SOFT SKILLS

Effective collaboration

INDUSTRY KNOWLEDGE

Artificial Intelligence and Machine Learning

EXPERIENCE

Professional or project experience in software engineering

The Fintech Job Report: Technology is eating finance

IT & Operations

The Ideal Fintech Candidate

HARD SKILLS
Network administration

MINDSET
Problem solver

SOFT SKILLS
Excellent communication

INDUSTRY KNOWLEDGE
Fintech acumen

EXPERIENCE
Professional experience in a similar role

The Fintech Job Report: Technology is eating finance

Data Science

The Ideal Fintech Candidate

HARD SKILLS

Data analysis and visualisation

MINDSET

Ability to work in a fast-paced environment

SOFT SKILLS

Cross-functional collaboration

INDUSTRY KNOWLEDGE

Artificial Intelligence and Machine Learning

EXPERIENCE

Professional or project experience

Product Management

The Ideal Fintech Candidate

HARD SKILLS

 Customer research methodologies

MINDSET

 Customer centricity and empathy

SOFT SKILLS

 Written and verbal communication

INDUSTRY KNOWLEDGE

 Fintech Acumen

EXPERIENCE

 Professional experience in a comparable role

Design
The Ideal Fintech Candidate

HARD SKILLS

 Digital designing tools

MINDSET

 Creativity and user-centricity

SOFT SKILLS

 Organization and time management

INDUSTRY KNOWLEDGE

 Fintech acumen

EXPERIENCE

 Professional or project experience

Marketing & Communications

The Ideal Fintech Candidate

HARD SKILLS

Search Engine Optimisation

MINDSET

Comfortable with ambiguity

SOFT SKILLS

Collaboration and communication

INDUSTRY KNOWLEDGE

Fintech acumen

EXPERIENCE

Portfolio or previous work

Sales & Business Development

The Ideal Fintech Candidate

HARD SKILLS

 Sales and marketing

MINDSET

 Entrepreneurial mindset

SOFT SKILLS

 Written and verbal communication

INDUSTRY KNOWLEDGE

 Fintech acumen

EXPERIENCE

 Experience in a similar role and relevant industry

The Fintech Job Report: Technology is eating finance

Partnerships

The Ideal Fintech Candidate

HARD SKILLS

Sales and business development

MINDSET

Ability to deal with uncertainty

SOFT SKILLS

Communication skills

INDUSTRY KNOWLEDGE

Fintech acumen

EXPERIENCE

Extensive professional experience in a comparable position

Risk & Compliance

The Ideal Fintech Candidate

HARD SKILLS

Legislations and regulations

MINDSET

Analytical and detail oriented

SOFT SKILLS

Multi-tasking and time management

INDUSTRY KNOWLEDGE

Fintech and business acumen

EXPERIENCE

Work experience in relevant industry

The Fintech Job Report: Technology is eating finance

Core Business Finance

The Ideal Fintech Candidate

HARD SKILLS

 Solid foundation of financial theory

MINDSET

 Analytical and problem solving

SOFT SKILLS

 Presentations and written communication

INDUSTRY KNOWLEDGE

 Fintech and business acumen

EXPERIENCE

 Experience in a similar role

The Fintech Job Report: Technology is eating finance

Jobs in Fintech and the Required Skills

Engineering Roles
The Fintech Job Report

Engineering

Essential roles for digital companies

Given the fact that Fintech services rely heavily on software and technology, engineers play a significant role in the industry. They are in charge of creating, developing, testing and maintaining software, as well as generating software ideas and communicating with necessary stakeholders to understand their requirements. Engineers are the pillars of a Fintech company and therefore it is, and will continue to, be one of the most abundant positions on the Fintech job market.

On average, software engineers in Fintech need to have previous experience in similar roles. Depending on the seniority of the position, 2-10 years of work experience might be needed. Computer science degrees are sometimes required, especially when it comes to more junior positions. However, for senior and principal roles, recruiters mostly base their decisions on the experiences and professional achievements of the candidate. Entry level positions or internships are less common in the industry and typically a minimum of 2 years of experience is required.

Software engineering positions are also very common in Big Tech companies. The nature of the job is similar to what we have seen in Fintech so transitioning between these two industries should be quite straightforward. The main difference is that there are more entry-level opportunities in Tech, making it more ideal for students and young professionals.

Experience with programming languages such as JavaScript, Python, PHP, Ruby, HTML or CSS is crucial. Knowledge of infrastructures, databases, platforms or API are common must-haves. It is also important to note that soft skills are equally as sought-after. Software engineers usually work in teams, so being collaborative and having good communication skills are key to succeeding in this role.

Engineering

HARD SKILLS

- Programming languages: JavaScript, Python, Ruby, PHP HTML and CSS are the most common
- Node.js
- Databases and infrastructures
- Cloud platforms (AWS, GCP)
- APIs

SOFT SKILLS

- Collaboration (within a team and cross-functionally)
- Effective communication
- Teamwork
- Mentoring (more senior positions)

MINDSET

- Problem solver
- Innovative
- Proactive and takes ownership
- Self learner
- Customer and user empathy

EXPERIENCE AND INDUSTRY KNOWLEDGE

- Prior software engineering experience is commonly required
- Professional and/or project experience
- Computer science degree: undergraduate level is usually sufficient
- Fintech acumen
- Knowledge of AI and Machine Learning

Engineering- Front End

| Engineering Roles

Description

Front End engineers work on the product, user-facing code and its architecture to enhance user experience. Ultimately, Front End engineers are responsible for the look and feel of the product.

For this reason, not only do they have a strong engineering background (modern web-front end technologies), but they also need to partner and collaborate with designers, product managers and have a passion for customer service.

Analysis

This is typically not an entry level position and generally requires some experience with JavaScript and other modern Front End frameworks, as well as a degree in Computer Science.

It's a crucial role for Fintech companies given that their selling point is often the seamless user experience compared to traditional banks. Front End engineers provide the framework to maintain brand consistency across the firm product, so they work closely with Back-end engineers and UX/UI designers.

Top Skills

- JavaScript
- HTML, CSS
- Public Github

Experience

- Knowledge of modern Front End tech stacks
- Coding experience (JavaScript, HTML, CSS, Typescript…)
- Building web apps and applications
- Passion for customer experience
- Interested in design
- Degree: Computer Science, STEM

Software Engineer, Front End

➢ *Work with engineers across the company to build new features and products*
➢ *Work side-by-side with user facing teams to best understand the needs of our customers*
➢ *Design and implement experiments to improve our customer's experiences*

The Fintech Job Report: Technology is eating finance

Engineering - Back End

| Engineering Roles

Description

A Back End Engineer is responsible for the integration of user-facing elements developed by Front End developers with server side logic.

Typical activities include optimising applications to improve scalability, writing server scripts and APIs, designing and applying data storage solutions and ensuring the implementation of security and data protection.

Analysis

Back End Engineers typically possess a degree in Computer Science and are proficient in Back End coding platforms such as PHP, Python, Ruby, Java, JavaScript. They also need a basic understanding of Front End technologies to work closely with Front End developers.

This is a crucial role as it's responsible for designing the infrastructure of the main product that typically has to accommodate for several layers of security or complex technologies such as blockchains.

Top Skills

- Ruby, Python, PHP, Java
- Cloud platforms
- APIs

Experience

- Familiarity with servers
- Common Back End languages: Python, PHP, Ruby and Java)
- Debugging experience
- DBMS
- Experience using cloud providers (e.g.: AWS)
- Knowledge of Front End stack
- Degree: Computer Science, STEM

Senior Back End Developer

➤ *Work within a specific problem space critical to Klarna's current needs*
➤ *Design, develop and deploy Back End services with a focus on scalability, high availability and low latency*

Klarna.

The Fintech Job Report: Technology is eating finance

Engineering - Full Stack

| Engineering Roles

Description

A Full Stack Engineer works both with the server side of the product (Backend) and the client side (Front End). This means that Full Stack Engineers possess great coding skills across multiple areas, from the architecture side of the product to the design/ UI / UX side.

In Fintech companies they work across multiple areas such as Product, Customer Service, Design, Marketing or Compliance.

Analysis

Given the level of experience necessary to cover both Back End and Front End, this is rarely an entry role. It requires great communication skills to effectively interact with other departments and provide inputs to improve the product.

Previous Product/Design experience in Tech, Finance or Fintech companies is a prerequisite and in general, this role is highly valued given that they can close the gap between Front and Back End.

Top Skills

- JavaScript, Python, PHP, Ruby
- HTML, CSS
- Node.js

Experience

- Extensive experience in a similar role (Tech, Finance or Fintech)
- Programming languages: Java, Python, PHP
- Front End and backend technology stacks
- Experience with cloud computing platforms (AWS...)
- Degree: Computer Science, STEM

Senior Engineer - Full Stack

➢ Articulate a long term vision for growth engineering and infrastructure at Coinbase
➢ Work across the entire stack to build, test and ship new user facing products using modern tools like Node 8, ES6, PostgreSQL, React, Flow and Webpack

coinbase

The Fintech Job Report: Technology is eating finance

Platform Engineer

| Engineering Roles

Description

A Platform Engineer closes the gap between software and hardware, enabling developers to deploy softwares in a safer, easier and quicker way. Due to new technologies such as Cloud or APIs, this is an emerging role which was previously associated with Infrastructure Engineering.

They can be seen as intermediaries between Back End/Infrastructure Engineers and Frontend Engineers by providing infrastructure that increases their productivity.

Analysis

Typical tasks include automation of deployment processes, writing documentation for application developers, building platforms and APIs, unifying cloud and data-center observability or general feature enhancements.

This is a crucial role for many Fintech companies given the need to improve efficiency of processes, especially compared to traditional banks. Platform Engineers may work in areas such as Product, Risk and Compliance or Engineering.

Top Skills

- Cloud Platforms (AWS, GCS…)
- JavaScript: Java Database
- APIs

Experience

- Coding and computer programming
- CI/CD
- Experience with cloud providers
- APIs and product development
- Fullstack experience
- Platform development
- Degree: Computer Science, STEM

Frontend Platform Engineer

> *Design, build, evolve, and maintain the foundational frontend ecosystem and underlying tools used by all of Stripe's product engineering teams*
> *Own and drive changes that increase the productivity of Stripe engineers working on frontend applications*

The Fintech Job Report: Technology is eating finance

Machine Learning Engineer

| Engineering Roles

Description

Machine Learning Engineers apply Machine Learning (ML) tools to help Fintech companies in areas such as fraud detection, personalisation of user experience, profiling, interest rate optimisation, assessment of creditworthiness, improvement of the flow of money transactions and much more.

Machine learning techniques such as reinforcement learning, decision theory, deep learning, and optimisation theory can be used to dynamically minimise costs while maximising revenue.

Analysis

ML Engineers usually have an impressive academic background with MSc or PhD degrees. Typically, industry experience is also a requirement.

Due to the complexity of the subject, communication skills are often a strong differentiator in this specific role, as ML Engineers need to be able to share results and findings with a "non-technical" audience in Operations, Engineering or Product Management. Previous experience (professional or academic) with financial products is also highly preferred.

Top Skills

- ML Development
- Python, JavaScript
- Cloud Platforms (AWS, GCS…)

Experience

- Programming and coding
- Strong foundation in ML and AI
- Implementing and and optimising machine learning models
- Data engineering and analysis, statistical modeling
- Deep learning frameworks
- Degree: Computer Science, STEM

Machine Learning Engineer

> Build machine learning that detect risk activity in real time across our Seller's ecosystem
> Collaborate with business leaders, subject matter experts, and decision makers to optimise new products, features, policies, and models

Solutions Engineer

| Engineering Roles

Description

A Solutions Engineer works between clients and developers by translating customers' requests into product related features and functionality.

They are the first point of contact for the developers team and their role encompasses both technical and management related tasks. It is not an entry level job and it's a crucial role to ensure optimal customer satisfaction.

Analysis

Solutions Engineers have typically worked for a considerable amount of years in IT or Engineering roles and usually hold a Computer Science degree.

Communication and Organisational skills are crucial in this role. We see Solutions Engineers more commonly in Tech companies than Traditional Financial Institutions.

Top Skills

- **Python, JavaScript**
- **Sales**
- **Customer Empathy**

Experience

- Experience in a similar role
- HTML/CSS
- Programming and coding
- Implementing web technologies
- Sales/account management
- Degree: Computer Science, STEM

Solutions Engineer

➢ *Consult with new prospects, and existing partners at the enterprise level, providing best in class technical solutions designs*

➢ *Collaborate closely with internal teams to ensure all aspects of the launch are effectively managed*

Data Engineer

| Engineering Roles

Description

Data Engineers are responsible for a broad range of tasks such as analysis of trends in data sets, management of dashboards, data warehousing and development of frameworks for data quality measurement.

In order to develop algorithms to allow for easier access to raw data, Data Engineers need to understand the dynamics within the Fintech company. This often includes working closely with the Risk And Compliance, Finance, Business Development and IT & Operations.

Analysis

In addition to strong technical skills such as SQL, Databases and Cloud technologies, Data Engineers need to be able to communicate effectively in order to work across multiple departments.

This role is extremely important for Fintech companies given their data-driven approach. Usually, Data Engineers have a background in Computer Science, Engineering, or Applied Mathematics given that this role relies heavily on coding abilities. Prior experience with data-intensive applications is also a must-have.

Top Skills

- **Big Data tools: Spark, Kafka, Hive, NiFi**
- **Cloud Platforms**
- **Python, JavaScript**

Experience

- Experience in a similar role
- Programming and coding experience (e.g. SQL)
- Cloud experience
- Data architecture, solutions architecture
- CI/CD
- Machine Learning frameworks
- Degree: Computer Science, STEM

Data Engineer

➢ Maintaining and enhancing our core data infrastructure, ETL framework
➢ Complementing our data scientists by providing a reliable, secure, and maintainable modelling framework

Revolut

Security Engineer

| Engineering Roles

Description

Security Engineers supervise the infrastructure that allows Fintech companies to keep personal information confidential, and more broadly to identify and mitigate risks for clients and stakeholders.

They engage in a wide range of collaborations across departments (Risk and Compliance, Product, Finance, Operations, Customer Service) and implement practices to anticipate and prevent potential risks.

Analysis

Given the damage that data-breaches can cause, this is a very important role that typically deals with sensitive information. It requires not only strong coding competencies, but also an understanding of forensic practices. The ability to bring improvements to existing processes is crucial in a role that requires anticipating potential threats. Previous experience in Tech is valued as well as experience in security engineering oriented roles.

Top Skills

- Security Design and Engineering
- Security Simulation Software
- Cloud Platforms (AWS, GCS)

Experience

- Experience in a similar role
- Software development experience
- Knowledge about network and internet security
- Experience with cloud providers (AWS, Azure, GCP,...)
- Degree: Computer Science, STEM

Cloud Security Engineer

➢ *Configure and maintain the defensive infrastructure and ensure that all assets are hardened in line with Security Policies and standards*
➢ *Ensure that security and availability requirements are met*

The Fintech Job Report: Technology is eating finance

Jobs in Fintech and the Required Skills

IT & Operations Roles

The Fintech Job Report

IT & Operations

Essential roles for digital companies

IT & Operations support Fintech organisations to manage, monitor and maintain a company's infrastructure. They also refine the way IT approaches services, deployment and support to promote consistency, reliability and quality of service. This forms the day-to-day operations of the company including responding to user requests, monitoring and executing system backups.

Individuals working in IT & Operations may not require experience for joining some internships or entry level jobs, however, these positions are quite rare in Fintech. As one grows into the more experienced roles, evidence of professional achievements is required. 2-15 years of professional experience is a common prerequisite depending on the seniority of the position.

In Fintech, IT & Operations is a division which is essential, common and growing due to the mass technology in use for the companies and individuals in these fields. There are no significant differences in terms of responsibilities in comparison to banks or technology companies. However, the different software and industry knowledge required in these positions depends on the particular company and position.

Specific skill requirements for these positions vary however, typically, individuals in these roles have the ability and skills to deal with LAN administration, manage the servers, systems and software of the company, as well as prepare and maintain records of clients agreements and systems. Additionally, cross-functional collaboration and communication with individuals who have a different technical background is very common, therefore, active listening and an ability to explain complex matters simply are important factors for succeeding in this role.

IT & Operations

HARD SKILLS

- Network administration
- Device administration
- Service operations
- Experience in SQL, Python, Excel

SOFT SKILLS

- Explain complex problems in communication
- Cross functional collaboration
- Attention to detail
- Active listening skills
- Time management

MINDSET

- Identification and solving of problems
- Willing to learn
- Forward thinker
- Proactive

EXPERIENCE INDUSTRY KNOWLEDGE

- Prior experience in a similar role
- Experience with system installation, configuration and analysis
- Knowledge of networks
- Knowledge of data protection and legislation
- Degree in computer science, IT or relevant field
- Fintech acument

Consumer Operations

| IT & Operations

Description

Consumer Operations professionals create an environment to help a company improve customer experience by collaborating with different departments such as Customer Service, Risk and Compliance, Product and Marketing.

In Fintech companies they are typically expected to follow a data driven approach while possessing great analytical and interpersonal skills to better understand customer needs.

Analysis

Common requirements for this role is having relevant work experience within Service Operations or similar roles in Tech, Consulting or Financial Services companies. It is also necessary to possess a strong understanding of the business model in the Fintech company. Multitasking, a great attention to detail and strong analytical skills are also crucial in this position.

Top Skills

- **Microsoft Excel**
- **SQL**
- **Detail-oriented**

Experience

- Excel and SQL skills
- Data visualisation (Tableau)
- Experience in a financial services / payments company
- Undergraduate degree in finance/ operations
- Experience working on business operations, risk and fraud management

---

Consumer Operations Associate

➢ *Analyse and help implement fraud and risk management rules and policies*
➢ *Work with product team and engineers to continuously improve operations and automate processes and launch new features/services*

Insurance Operations

| IT & Operations

Description

An Insurance Operations professional develops foundational processes for the company, scaling operations while bringing technical and operational improvements to claims processes and ensuring compliance, improving scalability, and managing risks. A variety of technical skills may be a prerequisite for this position such as coding skills or databases.

Top Skills

- Data analysis
- Microsoft Excel or Google Sheets
- Communication skills

Analysis

Previous working experience in a similar role within industries such as Operations, Health Insurance, Data Analysis, Engineering or Consulting is highly valuable. Data Analysis skills are also expected (Excel, Python, SQL), as well as experience in developing project plans, coordinating with internal and external stakeholders and optimising workflows.

Experience

- Experience in IT services
- Experience in Data services
- Database management
- Communication skills
- Finance and insurance knowledge

Insurance Operations - Claims

> *Develop processes for scaling claims operations and summarise data and operations into clear explanations*
> *Lead team to surface data, process, and technology issues*

Fraud Operations

| IT & Operations

Description

Fraud Operations Specialists investigate suspicious orders or transactions and proactively minimise the criminal behaviors that the company and its customers are facing.

In Fintech companies this is typically a data-driven role that needs to take legislative changes and regulations into consideration.

Analysis

Previous experience for this role includes relevant work experience within Customer Service, Fraud Operations or Service Delivery Management. Analytical and Problem Solving skills are highly valued as well as Stakeholder Management.

A bachelor's degree is sometimes required, however, having practical and professional experiences is the number one criterion for Fintech employers.

Top Skills

- Fraud or Customer Service experience
- Communication skills
- Analytical mindset

Experience

- Fraud/risk experience in Fintech industry
- Basic knowledge of banking and financial industry regulations
- Technical knowledge of various systems related to fraud and AML, etc.
- Bachelor's degree is sometimes required
- Experience in fraud or customer service experience

Fraud Operations Team Lead

- Owning processes and routines within the Fraud Operations team scope
- Drive improvements both on a process/routine level, as well as systems level, working closely with relevant internal stakeholders in the wider fraud group

The Fintech Job Report: Technology is eating finance

Business Operations

| IT & Operations

Description

Business Operation Professionals are cross-functional team members that ensure departments such as Customer Service or Product achieve operational excellence. They support and facilitate collaborations across multiple divisions while optimising procedures and workflow thanks to a data-driven approach. They also establish company policies to ensure an optimal customer satisfaction.

Analysis

Previous experience for this role includes relevant work experience within Consulting, Financial Services and Tech firms, especially in Operations and Project Management. Crucial skills include experience in performing analysis and presenting it, familiarity with business metrics, databases, data analysis skills, organisational skills and leadership.

Top Skills

- SQL, Python, R
- Microsoft Suite and G-Suite
- Communication skills

Experience

- Company experience in Fintech, business operations or investor relations
- G-Suite and Microsoft Office Suite
- SQL/Python/R
- Bachelor's degree: Engineering, Math, computer Science, Economic or Finance
- Experience in investment banking, management consulting or private equity

---

Business Operations Associate

➢ *Monitor and analyse ongoing business operations via qualitative and quantitative methods to report on progress, KPIs, SLAs, and build dashboards, reports, and ad hoc analyses*

➢ *Design and implement scalable cross functional operational and technical solutions*

The Fintech Job Report: Technology is eating finance

Operational Risk

| IT & Operations

Description

Operational Risk professionals design and manage procedures to mitigate risks arising from core operations, people, and systems. They scale regulatory operations and optimise operations to meet regulatory obligations.

Their focus is on people development, regulations adherence, workflow efficiency management, resource allocation, fraud and risk mitigation.This is a crucial role given the burden that compliance related issues can cause to an agile Fintech company.

Analysis

Previous experience for this role includes relevant work experience within Operations especially in an Insurance/Financial Services or regulated company.

Given the focus on fraud, Data Analysis skills are also required (Excel, SQL, Python) as well as experience in knowledge management processes, strategic planning and workflow planning management.

Top Skills

- Risk management
- Problem solving
- Communication skills

Experience

- Experience in Operational risk governance, Scenario analysis, KRIs and Risk appetite
- Prior experience in Fintech, Financial services or banking
- Financial risk or operational risk related certifications/qualifications are advantageous

---

Operational Risk Analyst

➢ *Facilitate and coordinate regular operational risk self-assessment carried out by business functions*
➢ *Assist In risk assessment, scenario analysis and internal control audit to address potential risks*

The Fintech Job Report: Technology is eating finance

Jobs in Fintech and the Required Skills

Data Science Roles

The Fintech Job Report

Data Science

Essential roles for digital companies

The growth of the Fintech industry has been powered by technological advancements such as Big Data. Large amounts of data and the ability to process them are one of the main competitive advantages that Fintech companies have, as it allows them to have a deep understanding of their customer base, which in turn can lead to smarter business decisions that put customer experience first.

Data scientists are in charge of analysing, processing and modelling these large sets of structured and unstructured data, as well as extracting relevant information to the organisation. Given the fact that Fintech is such a data-driven industry, the various roles of data scientists are crucial to the running and success of these companies.

Previous experiences in Data Science, Business Analytics or even Software Engineering are highly desirable. 10+ years of experience is a typical requirement for managerial or senior roles. A university degree in a quantitative subject such as Computer Science, Engineering, Mathematics or Statistics is required by some companies. However, certain organisations focus only on the professional experiences and achievements of the candidate. A strong knowledge of Finance is not necessary, nonetheless, an interest in learning about Finance and Fintech is desirable.

Data Science job roles are abundant in both traditional financial institutions as well as tech companies. In general, the nature of the job is similar across these three industries, so transitioning into Fintech from banking or a tech company is relatively straightforward.

Knowledge of database operation, data visualisation tools and cloud platforms are some of the main requirements. A strong foundation of mathematics, specifically statistics, is also crucial. The most commonly required programming languages are R, Python and SQL. Besides technical skills, communication, good presentation skills, collaboration and problem solving are also traits that a successful candidate should possess.

Data Science

HARD SKILLS

- Database operations
- Data visualisation tools (Tableau, Power BI...)
- Programming languages (R, Python, SQL)
- Cloud platforms (AWS, GCP...)
- Statistics

SOFT SKILLS

- Communication
- Cross-functional collaboration
- Presentation skills

MINDSET

- Problem Solving
- Proactivity
- Detail oriented and analytical
- Working in a fast-paced environment

EXPERIENCE AND INDUSTRY KNOWLEDGE

- Software engineering, business analytics or data science
- Professional and/or project experience
- Degree: Computer Science, Engineering, Mathematics, Statistics or any other quantitative discipline
- Fintech acumen

Data Analyst

| Data Science

Description

A Data Analyst cleans raw data, analyses them with a variety of statistical tools, validates insights extracted from the datasets and provides data-driven recommendations.

In Fintech companies, this role is present in areas such as Risk and Compliance (e.g. fraud detection) or Finance (e.g. credit worthiness) but could also appear in divisions such as Product, Marketing, Customer Success, Engineering, HR or Operations.

Analysis

Relevant experience could come from a similar role in e-Commerce, Banking, Consulting, Tech or Fraud Investigation. The level of necessary experience varies, it can therefore be an entry-level position as well. Knowledge of financial concepts can be useful, especially within Risk and Compliance, but it's often not a prerequisite.

As Data Analysts operate in teams, the ability to synthesise and communicate complex information effectively is often an important prerequisite.

Top Skills

- Data visualisation (Tableau, Power BI)
- R, Python, SQL
- Database operation

Experience

- Experience managing large sets of complex data
- Statistics (regression, A/B testing)
- Data visualisation platforms (Tableau, Power BI)
- Analytical and modelling experience
- Degree: Computer Science, Mathematics, Statistics, Engineering, Finance

Senior Data Analyst

➢ *Conduct data analysis, generate actionable insights and make recommendations for improving, developing and launching products*
➢ *Collaborate with engineering teams and stakeholders to build key datasets and data pipelines using Python/ETL frameworks*

Data Engineer

| Data Science

Description

Data Engineers implement data solutions to satisfy business needs and their scale-up. Responsibilities include building data, ML, statistical and design models to support various teams such as Customer Support, Compliance, Operations, Product, Marketing or Sales And Business Development. Fintech companies use Data Engineers especially to provide frameworks to improve internal processes.

Analysis

Prerequisites for this role may include knowledge of various programming languages, databases (Hive/Hadoop, Teradata, SQL, etc.), data visualisation technologies (e.g. Tableau), compliance tools, data pipelines and data warehouse architectures.

Relevant experience can be acquired through similar roles in Data Engineering, Data Warehousing, Data Analysis or Infrastructure Engineering. Crucial abilities for this role include relationship building with business partners, presentation, communication and organisational skills.

Top Skills

- Python, R
- Big Data tools (Spark, Kafka, Hive, NiFi)
- AWS and cloud platforms

Experience

- Software engineering experience
- Data pipeline analytics
- Database operations
- Knowledge of data warehouse architectures, ETL, reporting/ analytic tools and data security
- Cloud platforms
- Degree: Computer Science, Engineering, Mathematics or any IT-related discipline

---

Data Engineer (New Grad)

➤ *Building, improving, maintaining data pipelines and foundational frameworks for data ingestion and data transformation*

➤ *Design and implement scalable and reliable backend infrastructure of the Data applications*

Data Quality Analyst

| Data Science

Description

Data Quality Analysts implement data quality frameworks, processes, procedures and guidelines across various company departments to monitor the quality of data from which Fintech companies take decisions.

This is extremely important, as often high volumes of data do not imply good quality data, so Data Quality Analysts ensure that the decision making process is smooth, consistent and of high quality. They often collaborate with database developers as well as the management team.

Analysis

Prerequisites for this role may include proficiency in various programming languages, databases, data visualisation technologies, data governance, data system platforms, practices or data management.

Relevant experience can be acquired through similar roles in Financial Services firms. Crucial abilities for this role include relationship building with business partners, presentation and organisational skills. This role requires working collaboratively across various teams to conduct root cause analysis for data quality issues that arise with critical data elements.

Top Skills

- **Data visualisation (Tableau, Power BI)**
- **Database languages (SQL)**
- **Statistical packages (Excel, SAS, SPSS...)**

Experience

- Relevant professional experiences in data analysis
- Proficiency in programming languages (SQL)
- Manipulating large datasets
- Knowledge of data governance and policy
- Data enrichment and quality assurance
- Degree: Computer Science or any other IT-related field

Senior Data Quality Analyst

➢ Work with large scale enterprise data warehouse, data integration, data migration and data quality verification
➢ Performing ETL testing and validating against product specifications for transformation logic, data completeness and data types

Big Data Engineer

| Data Science

Description

Big Data Engineers design scalable and high volume backend data processing systems such as cloud-based data storage or warehousing services. In order to deliver solutions that can scale, they work across different teams in Data, Engineering, Product and IT & Operations.

Fintech companies are often high-growth companies, hence they need to be able to efficiently manage high volumes of data very quickly, something that makes a scalable and fault tolerant data system crucial.

Analysis

Prerequisites for this role may include proficiency in various programming languages, engines for large scale data processing (Hadoop, Spark, Scala), databases and knowledge of ML techniques.

Communication skills and critical/data-driven thinking are also key requirements in order to define problems, collect data, establish facts, and draw valid conclusions. Experience with data warehousing architecture and data modeling are also common requirements.

Top Skills

- Spark, Kafka, Hive, NiFi
- SQL, NoSQL
- Hadoop, Spark, Scala

Experience

- Software engineering or data experience
- Using public clouds (AWS, Azure, GCP,...)
- Database operations
- Data movement techniques
- Shell scripting experience
- Fundamentals of data structures and algorithms
- Degree: Computer Science, Engineering or equivalent

Engineer – Big Data Infrastructure

> *Be involved in the entire product lifecycle - from ideation to building, deploying and continual improvement of the platform feature set*
> *Design functionality, architect systems, instrument observability, establish and uphold data quality standards*

The Fintech Job Report: Technology is eating finance

Data Scientist

| Data Science

Description

Data Scientists transform raw data into valuable recommendations used by Fintech firms to grow and optimise processes. They also work on new ways of analysing data and produce BI solutions that allow for a wide variety of stakeholders to understand value measurement.

In Fintech companies they often act as an interface between "high tech" teams (e.g. Machine Learning team) and the broader business.

Analysis

Prerequisites for this role may include proficiency in various programming languages, databases and knowledge of ML techniques. Communication and presentation skills are vital since Data Scientists often need to explain technical data to a variety of executives and stakeholders.

Relevant work experience can be accumulated in fields such as quantitative analytics, data science, and analytical consulting within Tech or Finance companies.

Top Skills

- Data Visualisation (Tableau, Power BI)
- Data modelling
- Communication and Presentation

Experience

- Work experience in quantitative analytics, data science or similar field
- Manipulating raw data sets
- SQL, Python
- Cloud platforms
- Data visualisation, dashboards and reports
- Degree: Computer Science, Engineering, Statistics, Mathematics or equivalent

Data Scientist

➢ Mine and analyse data from company databases to drive optimisation and improvement of product
➢ Identify and integrate new datasets that can be leveraged through our product capabilities

The Fintech Job Report: Technology is eating finance

Analytics Manager

| Data Science

Description

An Analytics Manager transforms raw data into actionable business insights through the implementation of procedures within data analysis, reporting and analytics solutions. In Fintech companies, this role could appear in areas such as Operations, Product, Risk (e.g. Fraud) and Compliance, Finance, Marketing, Customer Success or Engineering.

Analysis

An Analytics Manager is expected to possess a skill set close to one of a Data Analyst, which includes proficiency with databases, statistical techniques and various programming languages. In addition, an Analytics Manager needs to have a sound understanding of the Fintech companies business model in order to develop strategies that bring tangible insights, as well as the ability to communicate these insights to the stakeholders involved. Often, an Analytics Manager leads a team of Data Scientists or Data Analysts.

Top Skills

- Data extraction and manipulation
- Database operations
- Python, R

Experience

- Data analysis and reporting experience
- Business intelligence tools
- Data visualisation tools
- Programming experience (R, SQL, Python)
- Knowledge of statistical techniques
- Leadership experience
- Degree: Computer Science, Engineering...

Analytics Manager – Product

- ➢ *Represent Data Analytics as a subject-matter expert in cross-functional initiatives*
- ➢ *Enable cross-functional partners to monitor and take actions based on the output of automated reports and dashboards tracking key metrics and business drivers*

Data Automation Developer

| Data Science

Description

RPA (Robotic process automation) Developers design, implement and maintain process automations to optimise the product or increase efficiency within a certain department. They work across different business areas such as Product or Operations and often produce process documentation to outline bad and good practices. In Fintech companies this role can help improve the product faster while ensuring a seamless user experience.

Analysis

Prerequisites for this role may include proficiency in various programming languages, databases and knowledge of ML techniques. Organisational skills and communication are key requirements for this role given that RPA Developers work closely with the Product team.

Relevant degrees include Computer Engineering, Mathematics, Management Information Systems while experience with Software Development or RPA technologies is highly desirable.

Top Skills

- Machine Learning and AI
- Java, Python, .NET
- Database operations

Experience

- Programming and coding experience
- Experiences with databases (SQL, NoSQL)
- Automation tools (UiPath, Ui Automation, Blue Prism)
- RDBMS
- Application integration
- Degree: Computer Science, Engineering or equivalent quantitative discipline

---

RPA Developer

- ➢ Develop automation workflows with UiPath Studio
- ➢ Learn and utilise new exciting technologies and how they integrate with UiPath
- ➢ Implement internal automations in order to improve the business processes used throughout the company

Business Intelligence Analyst

| Data Science

Description

Business Intelligence Analysts leverage business intelligence, data science, analytics and ML to translate business questions into structured analysis and recommendations. Their goal is to develop data-driven solutions that increase efficiency across business areas such as Product, IT & Operations, Marketing, HR and Finance. In Fintech companies, they help drive decision making based on user behaviours and feedback since the in-person interactions are often minimised.

Analysis

Prerequisites for this role may include proficiency in various programming languages, databases and data visualisation technologies. Relevant experience can be acquired through roles in Business Operations, Analytics, Data Science or Consulting.

Fintech companies are looking for individuals who are able to provide data driven solutions across the data layers of an organisation. This translates in the ability to work cross functionally with various teams and with external stakeholders. A passion for finding insights in data to drive change is also a desired quality.

Top Skills

- Python, SQL, R
- Dataset manipulation
- Database operations

Experience

- Experience in Business Analytics, Data Science, Business Operations or Consulting
- Data visualisation, data warehousing, predictive modeling
- Manipulating large and multi-dimensional data sets
- Degree: Engineering, Computer Science, Mathematics or any other equivalent quantitative discipline

---

Business Intelligence Associate

- ➢ *Deliver Data Excellence: Ensure a seamless data experience for core teams across the company*
- ➢ *Create Analytics: Support goal-setting across Lemonade. You'll create reports and dashboards to monitor KPIs to ensure teams are making intelligent and informed decisions*

Lemonade

The Fintech Job Report: Technology is eating finance

Data Infrastructure Analyst

| Data Science

Description

Software Engineers that work in Data Infrastructure design, build and maintain scalable systems for processing and analysis of large disparate data sets. They develop tools and applications to proactively measure data quality. They work with the Data and Engineering team to define best data management practices and typically possess extensive Tech skills.

Analysis

Prerequisites for this role may include experience in building large-scale backend systems, working knowledge of various programming languages, databases, and cloud tools. Relevant experience can be acquired through similar roles in Backend Engineering, Data Engineering, Data Analysis or Infrastructure Engineering. Crucial abilities for this role include attention to detail and willingness to work cross-functionally with various engineering and analytics teams.

Top Skills

- Scripting and development
- Relational and non-relational databases
- Backend software development

Experience

- Experience in Data Infrastructure and/or backend software development
- Developing and debugging in one or more programming language
- Experience with cloud environments (AWS, GCP...)
- Degree: Computer Science, Engineering or related technical field

---

Engineer – Data Infrastructures

- ➢ Design and build data infrastructure systems, services and tools to handle new Affirm products and business requirements
- ➢ Work cross-functionally with various engineering and analytics teams to identify and execute on new opportunities

The Fintech Job Report: Technology is eating finance

Jobs in Fintech and the Required Skills

Product Management Roles

The Fintech Job Report

Product Management

Essential roles for digital companies

The role of a product manager is very common in Fintech companies. This is a role that can be defined quite broadly and the specifics can change position to position, however, in general, they are in charge of overseeing the creation and development of Fintech services, as well as responsible for the whole lifecycle and the long-term strategy of the product. Typical tasks might include supervising the launch a new product, optimising customer experiences or analysing sentiments and implementing these findings into their product and services. Ultimately, no matter the nature of the task, a good product manager will always have their customers at the forefront of their mind.

This is rarely an entry-level position and past professional experiences in product management or comparable managerial roles is a common prerequisite. A bachelor's degree in a relevant field is sometimes required, however, for more senior roles such as Product Manager, professional achievements usually carry more weight.

Due to the fact that this role is heavily centred around the company's product, being familiar with the industry it operates in is a must-have. Those who have had previous experiences in Fintech, Tech, or Financial Services will have an easier time securing a role. Alternatively, being able to demonstrate a strong passion for the technological megatrends and the impact they have had on Finance is also valuable.

Product managers often work in cross-functional teams which might comprise of members from Design, Engineering or Marketing. For this reason, excellent collaboration and communication skills are very crucial in this role. Furthermore, due to the customer-centricity of this role, experience with customer research methodologies can be a major asset. Finally, technical skills such as data science or data analytics are common in roles that centre around Risk and Compliance or Data.

Product Management

HARD SKILLS

- Product analytics
- Product testing methodologies and tools
- Customer research methodologies
- Data analytics and data science are important in Risk and Compliance and Data centric roles

SOFT SKILLS

- Excellent communications skills
- Cross-functional collaboration
- Good organisational skills
- Stakeholder management
- Multitasking

MINDSET

- Customer centricity and user empathy
- Problem solver
- Leadership

EXPERIENCE AND INDUSTRY KNOWLEDGE

- Professional experience as a product manager
- Industry experience (Fintech, Tech, Financial Services)
- Demonstrate passion for the product and industry
- Bachelor's degree is rarely required, however, for more technical roles a degree in Engineering, Computer Science or any comparable course can be an advantage

Platform

| Product Management

Description

Product Managers for Platforms related roles oversee platform and product development from ideation through creation and execution. The job includes analysing customer feedback, building new strategies, creating new features on platforms - all with the aim to enhance user experience that is scalable and impactful. Product Managers work closely with individuals from Design, Engineering, Marketing and other cross-functional teams.

Analysis

Relevant experience can be acquired through similar roles in the E-commerce, Retail or Payment industry or while working with APIs & leading platform strategies. Crucial abilities for this role include relationship building with business partners, problem solving and organisational skills. This role often requires working collaboratively across various teams to share feedback and information.

Top Skills

- **Application Product Interface (API)**
- **Data Analytics**
- **Communication and Organisation Skills**

Experience

- Product Management experience for a platform-oriented product
- Experience working on products with developer facing interfaces (APIs, SDKs...)
- Used to rapid development cycles
- Bachelor's degree is sometimes required

Senior Product Manager, Platform

➢ *Create a well-thought-out product vision and strategy for the business and billing platform initiatives*
➢ *Create product specs, review business analysis for prioritisation, product performance metrics*

Core Business Finance

| Product Management

Description

Product Managers for roles relating to Core Business functions oversee and define product strategy, coordinate and execute core projects and optimise customers' experiences to drive growth. They work on scaling core business product operations to serve more customers, and explore new business opportunities. They set product vision and roadmap for APIs, toolkits and integrations to streamline operations and enhance customer experience.

Analysis

Relevant experience can be acquired through product management roles in the Software/Tech Industry or within the Financial Services industry. Familiarity with the core product is often a requirement (e.g. Payments, Credits, Underwriting) while the ability to collaborate and network across different divisions can help make the difference.

Top Skills

- Integration Tools
- A/B Testing
- Website Analytics

Experience

- Experience in Product Management in Finance, Fintech or Tech
- Product analytics, testing methodologies and data-backed decision processes
- Customer research methodologies (e.g. customer interviews, surveys, web analytics and A/B testing)

Product Manager

➢ *Drive product development and product solutions you are accountable for, as well as utilise qualitative and quantitative insights to develop hypotheses*
➢ *Develop an understanding of customers by conducting research, data analysis, customer interviews, and usability testing*

Risk & Compliance

| Product Management

Description

Product Managers for Risk & Compliance lead complex and dynamic programs that protect both customers and the company - preparing Risk Organisations for new product launches to advicing General Managers on financial risk loss management, to executing high impact, cross-functional projects. They make data-driven decisions, manage risks, and communicate extensively with key stakeholders across Risk And Compliance, Finance, Data and Product divisions.

Analysis

Prerequisites for this role may include relevant certifications or experience with product security. Relevant experience can be acquired through similar roles in security-related regulatory compliance for financial services or through related product management roles.

Crucial abilities for this role include leadership and stakeholder management, especially Engineers. This role often requires working collaboratively across various teams and the ability to understand customer needs.

Top Skills

- Regulations and AML compliance
- Written and verbal Communication
- Risk analysis

Experience

- Product management on a software platform product
- Experience with security-related regulatory compliance for financial services
- Relevant certifications (CISA, CISSP) could be beneficial
- Working cross functionally
- SQL or data science knowledge could be an added advantage

Product Compliance Manager

➢ Collaborating with key stakeholders to evaluate the potential compliance risks of any new or existing product, feature, or vertical

➢ Providing general AML/compliance advisory on behalf of the broader Compliance function

Data

| Product Management

Description

Product Managers for Data work with Engineering, Data, and Customer Service to plan for current and future projects that leverage the flow of data and aim to standardise key performance indicators. They often partner with Product Operations to ensure smooth processes and an efficient deployment of resources. In order to be able to interface with Engineering and Data divisions, a well rounded technical background is often required.

Analysis

Prerequisites for this role may include proficiency in various programming languages, databases and ML techniques. Relevant experience can be acquired through similar roles in Data Analysis, ML or other technical product management roles in high-growth tech environments. Other must-haves are: excellent decision making, curiosity, passion for the firm's product and ability to focus on the problem at hand. This role often requires working collaboratively across various teams and proactiveness.

Top Skills

- Data analytics and data science
- Communication skills
- Programming

Experience

Experience in Product Management

Data Science and Analytics

Working in a cross-functional environment

Degree: Engineering, Computer Science, Statistics, Mathematics, Economics (up to Masters or PhD)

Lead Product Manager, Data Platform

➢ Help define the product vision and strategy, and define and own the roadmap for the Data Platform teams that power all of our product ecosystem

➢ Support a cross-functional team of engineers, designers, and data scientists

Wealthsimple

The Fintech Job Report: Technology is eating finance

Jobs in Fintech and the Required Skills

Design Roles

The Fintech Job Report

Design

Essential roles for digital companies

The role of a designer can vary a lot as they play a crucial part in many areas of a Fintech company's operations. They can be in charge of creating and iterating the design of a product, producing digital content such as social media posts, videos, infographics or even looking after the User Experience (UX) aspect of the service. Designers play a significant role as, besides the functionalities of the product, the visual aspect of Fintech services and its marketing materials can have an enormous impact on customer perception and in turn acquisition.

Requirements for a design position vary based on the nature of the role as well as seniority; however, typically past professional or project experiences are highly valued. Bachelor degrees in creative disciplines such as Design can be beneficial, but are outweighed by practical experiences, especially in more senior positions. Submitting a portfolio of any relevant work is a common practice.

An interest and knowledge of Fintech is a definite must-have, as a designer should be able to tailor their work to this industry; however, experience working in Fintech, Finance or Technology is not a usual prerequisite. Graduate schemes or internship roles are very rare in Fintech; however, some of the positions do not require extensive professional experience. Students or young professionals who have pursued their designing interest through personal projects can still be eligible to apply for more junior roles.

Designers usually work on multiple projects and often work remotely, so good time management skills and effective communication is essential. Experience using digital designing tools such as Figma, Sketch, Adobe Photoshop or InVision are common requirements. Video creation and editing skills can be of relevance as well.

Design

HARD SKILLS

- Digital designing tools (Sketch, Figma, Adobe Photoshop, InVision, Canva Pro…)
- Creating and editing videos
- Photography
- Typography
- Microsoft Office Suite
- UX/UI

SOFT SKILLS

- Excellent collaboration and communication skills
- Time management
- Organisation
- Project management

MINDSET

- Creativity
- User-centricity
- Strategic

EXPERIENCE AND INDUSTRY KNOWLEDGE

- Professional or project experience
- Portfolio of previous relevant work
- A university degree is a rare requirement, however, a bachelor's degree in Design or any comparable creative discipline could be an advantage
- An interest in the industry and knowledge of the most recent Fintech trends

Product Designer

| Design

Description

Product Designers partner with other stakeholders, as well as use their designing skills and business knowledge, to execute exceptional design solutions at scale. They work closely with Product Managers, Engineers and UX Writers to deliver great consumer experiences.

Top Skills

- Modern design tools e.g Figma
- Competent in prototyping tools
- UX ability and product thinking

Analysis

This is usually not an entry-level position and requires professional design experience in areas such as consumer facing mobile and web applications. A bachelor's degree in HCI, Design, Architecture or a related field can be a prerequisite. However, most companies assess their candidates based on relevant experiences or projects.

Experience

Professional design experience

Have experience in working with multi-disciplinary teams in iterative product development cycles

Designing tools such as Figma, Sketch etc.

Bachelor's degree in Design can be beneficial and is sometimes a requirement

---

Product Designer

➤ *Design usable, accessible and engaging user experiences for Visa's digital product line*
➤ *Be responsible for developing elegant and simple experiences that help solve complex business and design challenges*

The Fintech Job Report: Technology is eating finance

Content Designer

| Design

Description

A Content Designer is in charge of creating digital content such as social media posts, emails, blog assets, infographics or digital assets for websites. However, in Fintech, they are responsible for creating content using principles, frameworks, product flows and in-product messaging across mobile and web products. They need to collaborate with other content designers and use data from consumers and merchants to collaborate on product strategy and deliver on experience design for the brand's products.

Analysis

A position in content design varies from entry level with 2+ years of experience to 8+ years combined experience for more senior roles. Knowledge of digital design tools such as Adobe Photoshop, Illustrator, Sketch or Figma are common. Animation tools like Motion Graphics, Adobe Animate or Sparks are usual prerequisites and are nice to have. Work at a Fintech company can be very fast-paced, so time management skills and the ability to multitask and work on numerous projects is also an important attribute.

Top Skills

- Sketch, Figma, Photoshop
- MS Office Suite
- Writing and editing skills

Experience

Experience using digital designing tools such as Sketch, Figma, Photoshop, Canva Pro, InVision, Adobe Illustrator

Previous UX writing work

Experience managing multiple projects

Bachelor's degree: Journalism, Communications, Marketing, Design...

Product Content Writer

➢ *Understand how content fits within the overall user experience, the goals and objectives, and figure out how to best create content to meet these*
➢ *Understand the needs of our diverse user base and the impact this has on how content needs to be created and presented*

The Fintech Job Report: Technology is eating finance

Art Director

| Design

Description

Art Directors are responsible for the look and feel of the company's marketing materials. Ultimately, they are in charge of creating campaigns that have an instant and positive impact on the customers. Designing concepts for the brand's communication with merchants, making digital content such as videos are also common tasks.

Analysis

This is usually not an entry level position and requires experience both from the creative agency side and also the brand side. Art Directors can be often seen collaborating with photographers, directors or set-engineers, so good communication and team working skills are also important. Submission of a portfolio which showcases the candidate's previous projects and work is essential for a role in design.

Top Skills

- Photoshop, InDesign, Illustrator, Sketch
- Videography, photography
- Typography

Experience

- Experience in design (in-house or agency)
- Portfolio of previous work
- Experience with a variety of mediums
- Digital designing tools such as Sketch, Figma, Photoshop, Canva Pro, InVision, Adobe Illustrator

---

Art Director

- ➢ Turn customer insights, marketing goals, and best practices into content that results in increased awareness, growth, and engagement
- ➢ Collaborate cross-functionally on projects across multiple channels and formats including ads, web, video, and animation

The Fintech Job Report: Technology is eating finance

UX Writer

| Design

Description

A UX Writer improves user experience by working closely with product managers, engineers and product designers to write content for web and mobile with a goal of guiding users through the product in the most effective and intuitive manner. They can also provide strategic and data-driven decisions on high priority projects and create consistent, new content which helps the business reach its objectives.

Analysis

Generally, for more entry level positions, 2+ years experience working in UX writing for digital products, apps or websites is required. However, for some senior roles, 5+ years of experience is required. The most fundamental skills of a UX writer is the ability to empathise with users and implement these insights into their work in the form of navigation items or error messages. Being data-driven is also a key part of being a UX Writer, as analysing the impact of the content is equally as important as creating it. Finally, the submission of a portfolio is a common requirement.

Top Skills

- Writing and communication skills
- Design processes
- UX research methods

Experience

- Professional experience working in a similar role for digital products, apps or websites
- Understanding of UX, design and usability best practices
- Portfolio of previous work (UX writing might be given instead if a sample of previous work is not provided)
- Knowledge of digital design tools is an asset, not an usual requirement

---

UX Writer

➢ Optimise in-product copy to best reflect user needs and brand experience
➢ Drive cohesive product narratives that solve real customer problems
➢ Work with multiple stakeholders from different backgrounds to define an in-product voice and tone

The Fintech Job Report: Technology is eating finance

UX Researcher

| Design

Description

A UX Researcher's main task is to understand consumers, their motivations, needs and wants. Their insights should be implemented when developing products that put user-centered design at its core. Cross-functional collaboration with engineers is also very common, so besides good team working skills, having general knowledge of technical jargon and concepts is very crucial. Finally, analysing both quantitative and qualitative data is central to the role.

Analysis

Relevant professional experiences as a UX Researcher in a digital company are common prerequisites, however, equivalent skills can be gained through various personal projects as well. A university degree is sometimes required, with the most desirable majors being Design, Psychology, Cognitive Sciences or any other research-intensive course. Knowledge of research methodologies, their weaknesses and scenarios in which they would be applied, is essential across the board.

Top Skills

- **Verbal and written communication**
- **Research methodologies**
- **Survey design and analysis**

Experience

- Past roles in User Experience, Design, Research or any other related field
- Experience working with financial services is an advantage
- Knowledge of various research methodologies and their weaknesses (qualitative interviews, surveys, ideation sessions, ethnographic field research)
- Testing digital products

Principal User Researcher

➢ Identify emerging opportunities for improving user experience
➢ Build new systems that help us better understand our user experience
➢ Identify the root causes of wider customer experience issues and help tackle them

Jobs in Fintech and the Required Skills

Marketing & Communications Roles

The Fintech Job Report

Marketing & Communications

Essential roles for digital companies

The Marketing and Communications team are responsible for the activities that engage with the Fintech's current and potential customers, building a strong relationship with them, as well as promoting the product to a wider audience. The nature of this role can vary greatly, from more creative tasks, such as copywriting, creating digital marketing campaigns and materials, to more analytical tasks, such as designing marketing automation flows or CRM integration.

Typically, previous extracurricular or professional experiences in a similar position is required. A bachelor's degree in Marketing, Communications, or any comparable field can be an asset; however, an academic qualification is seldom necessary. As you progress in your career and aim for more senior positions, these qualifications will become less important. There might not be many internship or graduate schemes available in Fintech; however, some of the positions do not require extensive professional experience in the field. Past experiences with Fintech, Finance or Technology are favoured although, a proven interest and passion for the industry is usually substantial, as a familiarity with Fintech will ultimately help you to tailor your work to the right audience.

Communications, and especially marketing, are disciplines that require both creativity and technical skills. Typical requirements are strong writing and editing skills, excellent knowledge of marketing automation tools, web analytics, Microsoft Suite, Sketch or Adobe Creative Suite. For some positions, technical skills such as HTML/CSS or CRM tools like Braze are prerequisites. Finally, soft skills such as effective communication, good presentation skills and cross-functional collaboration are highly desirable.

Marketing & Communications

HARD SKILLS

- Strong and flexible writing and copywriting skills
- Ability to write and create for multiple channels
- Marketing automation
- Web analytics
- Adobe Creative Suite
- Microsoft Suite

SOFT SKILLS

- Communication
- Collaboration in team and cross-functionally
- Presentation skills
- Multi-tasking

MINDSET

- Creative
- Analytical
- Customer-centric
- Attention to detail
- Ability to deal with ambiguity

EXPERIENCE AND INDUSTRY KNOWLEDGE

- Project or professional experience
- Portfolio or example of previous work
- Bachelor's degree in Marketing or Communications can be an asset; however, not necessary
- Understanding of Fintech and the most important trends of the industry

Growth Marketer

| Marketing and Communications

Description

The role of a growth marketer is becoming increasingly more relevant in Fintech. Unlike traditional marketers, who focus just on the top of the funnel, growth marketers focus on the entire funnel and engage with the entire customer lifecycle in an effort to improve conversion rates.

Growth marketing is also all about iterating, experimenting and adapting to the changing preferences of the customer.

Analysis

This is typically not an entry-level position and requires previous professional experiences in a similar role. Growth marketing is a highly analytical and data-driven for this reason, methods such as A/B testing are also commonly used.

Given the strategic nature of the role, cross-functional collaboration is also very common. As a growth marketer, you can expect to work with teams which work on different aspects of the business, such as Product or Sales.

Top Skills

- A/B testing
- Data analysis
- Conversion rate optimisation

Experience

- Relevant professional experience in a similar role
- Experience with the whole marketing process (ideation, design, execution and performance analysis)
- Data visualisation and analysis
- Passion for industry and knowledge of relevant Fintech sectors

---

Growth Marketing Manager

➢ *Proactively identify channel optimisation and growth opportunities, surfacing dependencies and blockers to the growth marketing team and cross-functional stakeholders*
➢ *Partner with internal and external creative teams to advance a creative learning agenda*

Communications

| Marketing and Communications

Description

The Communications team is responsible for driving awareness of the company to generate demand and revenue. Those with fewer years of experience assist with press lists, briefing documents and blog posts.

Senior managerial roles work closely with company management to drive corporate communications. They also work on content marketing strategies and are in charge of ensuring that the company has a strong presence in business, tech and financial media outlets.

Analysis

Prerequisites for this role will vary depending on seniority, however, having a relevant professional background is standard. For entry-level positions, these skills can be gained through extracurricular activities or projects. A bachelor's degree in communications or journalism could be an asset during the application process, however, it usually isn't a requirement.

Top Skills

- **Copywriting**
- **Writing and editing skills**
- **Microsoft Office Suite**

Experience

- Relevant experience in a PR agency or an in-house communications team
- Understanding of trends in technology/fintech communications
- Creating compelling and bold content
- Experience with various communication channels
- Relevant degrees: Communications, Journalism

Communications Manager

- Develop a media strategy that will ensure Ramp becomes recognised as a leader in fintech
- Manage relationship with our external PR agency and build brand awareness

The Fintech Job Report: Technology is eating finance

Copywriter

| Marketing and Communications

Description

Copywriting plays a crucial role in developing ideas and marketing communications. Such writing is used for channels like apps, emails and in performance marketing such as Facebook and Google Ads.

Copywriters tend to work alongside designers, marketing managers and PR specialists, therefore, cross-functional collaboration and effective communication are important skills for this role. This role is often remote, so effective time management is also essential.

Analysis

Copywriting is seldom an entry-level position in FinTech, therefore, previous professional experience in the field is usually required. An interest in UX and UX-writing is also beneficial. A university degree is not a common requirement, however, degrees in essay-based degrees such as English or History might be an asset. Instead of academic qualifications, employers will typically ask for examples of previous work. Finally, knowledge and interest in Fintech is highly desirable.

Top Skills

- **Flexible writing style**
- **Knowledge of multiple channels**
- **Strategic and tactical communication**

Experience

- Copywriting experience for Technology, Fintech or Financial Services companies
- Experience writing for various channels and formats
- Cross-functional collaboration as well as independent work
- Managing multiple projects at once

Copywriter

- ➢ Collaborate with our in-house creative team to develop new marketing campaigns
- ➢ Assist with writing corporate emails to employees, clients, and leads
- ➢ Research and write articles on Heart & Hustle, the SpotOn blog

The Fintech Job Report: Technology is eating finance

CRM

| Marketing and Communications

Description

Integrating Fintech with CRM is crucial to improve workflow efficiency and customer intelligence. CRM supports various business functions and improves pipeline visibility with use of the correct technology and marketing automation tools. Such activities within CRM include working on marketing campaigns and collaborating with growth teams design. Those with more experience tend to focus more on data and CRM analytics.

Analysis

Typically, a minimum of 2-3 years experience of working with CRM & Marketing Automation is required as well as a BA degree. A bachelor's degree in Information Technology, Business and Marketing or any other related fields is an advantage but fundamentally, a university degree is required regardless of the discipline.

Top Skills

- CRM tools (Braze, SFMC...)
- CRM Analytics
- A/B testing and other analytics tools

Experience

- Relevant CRM experience
- Basic HTML, CSS, SQL is a plus
- Experience with A/B testing
- CRM tools: Braze, SFMC/ExactTarget, Adobe/Marketo, CheetahMail, Dotdigital, Selligent, Hubspot
- CMS tools: Adobe, WordPress, Hubspot
- Bachelor's degree

Senior CRM Tech Manager

➢ *Setting up, manage and monitor customer segments, marketing and transactional messaging*
➢ *Technical implementation of email, push, weblayers and in-app messages*
➢ *Maximise 3rd party relationships to drive CRM platform innovation*

Performance Marketing

| Marketing and Communications

Description

Performance marketing involves executing and measuring digital marketing campaigns across various channels including social advertising, emails, or editorial articles to drive acquisition and new user growth. Performance marketing involves collaborating with those in Product, Engineering, and Designers to develop strategies to support the company's business and marketing goals.

Analysis

Prerequisites for performance marketing include at least 3+ years of experience designing for marketing campaigns with a Bachelor's degree or equivalent practical experience. Those in performance marketing have a strong understanding of analytics, testings and metrics, as well as a good knowledge of other markets.

Top Skills

- Sketch & the Adobe Creative Suite
- UX & design fundamentals
- Web analytics

Experience

- Extensive marketing experience
- Working cross-functionally
- Using both digital and offline channels
- Experience working for a Fintech or high-growth company
- Bachelor's degree in Marketing or equivalent subjects could be an asset

---

Growth Marketing Manager

➢ *Recruit, close, and coach influencers to create native content that drives massive results*
➢ *Lead performance marketing campaigns from idea to reporting across the acquisition, activation, and retention funnel*

The Fintech Job Report: Technology is eating finance

Marketing Automation

| Marketing and Communications

Description

This unique role involves designing and implementing marketing automation flows across multiple channels. The goal is to engage users at all stages of the user journey i.e onboarding, activation and loyalty. Typical daily tasks might include: creating or monitoring reports on lead creation, improving the demand generation process or ensuring and maintaining data quality.

Analysis

Prerequisites for entry level positions include 3+ years experience working within CRM & Marketing Automation and other analytical tools to ensure customer understanding and campaign results. For managerial roles, 5+ years of experience is usually required. A Bachelor's degree with a focus in Marketing, Information Systems is desirable but any discipline is acceptable.

Top Skills

- Marketing automation tools (Braze, Marketo...)
- Google Analytics, Salesforce
- HTML/CSS knowledge

Experience

- Experience working with CRM or marketing automation
- A/B multivariate testing
- CMS platforms
- Understanding of digital marketing
- Bachelor's degree in Marketing or Informations Systems might be required, however is not always necessary

---

Marketing Automation Manager

➢ Work with key stakeholders to develop new processes in Marketo
➢ Monitor and improve data flow in Marketo and between Marketo and Salesforce
➢ Monitor data quality in Marketo and work on data clean-up

Jobs in Fintech and the Required Skills

Sales & Business Development Roles

The Fintech Job Report

Sales & Business Development

Essential roles for digital companies

While Sales and Business Development roles are common in traditional banking sectors and technology companies, they play a vital role in Fintech companies, especially when it comes to those servicing niche markets.

These roles involve conducting thorough research on leads, engaging in proactive outreach, developing extensive knowledge of niche markets, taking on other key activities to help effectively qualify leads and growing company revenue. Day-to-day responsibilities of individuals in these positions include tracking new market trends, making product recommendations, proposing strategic partnerships, maintaining client relationships, as well as being involved in long-term growth strategies.

Individuals working in sales and business development do not need any formal training, however, having a proactive mindset and willingness to learn are fundamental traits. Having a formal university education is usually not necessary, although, some companies may look for individuals with a sales or marketing background. For more senior positions, 5-15 years of experience in the field are required.

Typical skills required in Sales and Business Development include: knowledge of B2B and B2C sales tactics, strong communication and interpersonal skills, as well as extensive knowledge of the company's products and services. Writing reports, presenting to clients and internal management is also very common, therefore, having good presentation and writing skills can also be assets for these types of positions. Finally, curiosity and the ability to keep track of the new advancements in Fintech, persuasion and persistence are highly valued as well.

Sales & Business Development

HARD SKILLS

- Technical skills for software such as CRM, Collaboration software
- Sales and marketing

SOFT SKILLS

- Cross functional collaboration
- Extensive knowledge on products and services
- Time management skills
- Communication and interpersonal skills
- Negotiation skills

MINDSET

- Entrepreneurial mindset
- Curiosity mindset
- Proactive

EXPERIENCE AND INDUSTRY KNOWLEDGE

- No formal education/ sales and marketing background/ Advanced degree such as masters, PhD
- Experience with B2B/B2C sales
- Software such as CRM databases, communication and collaboration software
- A deep understanding of the industry and the product

Enterprise Sales

| Sales and Business Development

Description

Enterprise Sales within Fintech involves generating new business opportunities and identifying specific prospects and partners to approach. Individuals in this role are also in charge of communicating the specific value proposition for their business to establish long-term successful partners. This is essentially a Sales position that involves large-scale corporate solutions.

Analysis

This is often not an entry level position, as some roles require 8 years or more of experience in a role selling complex enterprise software, technical infrastructure or a financial service. Experience in payments is also desirable and those working in enterprise sales tend to have an extensive network in retail banking or automotive financing industries.

Top Skills

- Cloud, CDN, IaaS
- Pipeline reporting, RFP proposals
- Collaborative skills
- Sales and marketing

Experience

- Experience in SaaS, IaaS, or PaaS sales
- Experience working with customers within a relevant industry
- Sales experience
- Demonstrated ability in hitting sales targets consecutively
- Experience with sales cycles

Enterprise Sales

➢ Acquiring merchants with multiple outlets
➢ Do presentation, follow-up, delivering demo of the solutions, negotiations and closing deals
➢ To be the face of MOKA and GoStore to merchants to build strong rapport, partnership and relationship

The Fintech Job Report: Technology is eating finance

Business Development

| Sales and Business Development

Description

Business Development revolves around building relationships with prospective customers, networking with partners and generating new opportunities for the company.

Unlike sales, those working within Business Development tend to focus on the long term goals rather than the short term ones. There tends to be a common misconception that Business Development and Sales are the two different terms for the same jobs, specifically in Fintech startups.

Analysis

This is an entry level position as a minimum of 1-3 years of experience in Sales Development, Lead Generation or Sales is required. For Business Ops, more experience is required (3-4 years). Prerequisites include a Bachelor's degree and a proven track record of exceeding high volume opportunity growth sales quotas in hyper-growth environments.

Top Skills

- Sales & marketing
- Software experience
- Communication skills

Experience

- Communication
- Commercial acumen
- Experience in Sales Development, Lead Generation or Sales
- Proven track record of exceeding high-volume opportunity generation/sales quotas in hyper-growth, goal-focused environments

---

Business Development Representative

- *Build opportunity pipeline by identifying key decision makers within target accounts using internal sales tools and other publicly available information*
- *Meet all sales and performance objectives including daily activity target, monthly meeting, and sales qualified leads quota*

The Fintech Job Report: Technology is eating finance

Sales Engineer

| Sales and Business Development

Description

Sales Engineers are responsible for providing technical leadership, consultation and guidance for users as well as implementing the company's products and solutions to other businesses.

Sales engineers often bridge the gap between product development and sales as it is necessary for them to be able to explain highly technical concepts and functions to sales representatives and potential customers in a user-friendly and relatable way.

Analysis

Typically, 3+ years experience in eCommerce, Fintech or in a payments industry is required and experience working in a technical or commercial client-facing role. Sales Engineers also collaborate with those working in Product, Sales, IT & Operations. Some companies may prefer a Bachelor's in Engineering, Computer Science or other related fields of study or educational backgrounds in science or businesses with relevant work experience.

Top Skills

- Web services/ API's and system integration methods
- B2B sales experience
- Communication Skills

Experience

- BSc or MSc in STEM field
- Tech background or product background with technical depth
- Written and verbal communication skills
- Experience in sales and marketing
- Experience working in Fintech, Start-up is advantageous

Analyst - Sales Engineer

➢ *Develop and maintain knowledge of Cybersource payment management platform solutions*
➢ *Generate and deliver solution presentations and product demonstrations in a customer-facing environment to a range of audiences including executives and engineers*

The Fintech Job Report: Technology is eating finance

Partner Sales

| Sales and Business Development

Description

For Partner Sales, an experienced background in developing strategy, identifying partners, negotiating agreements and rapidly scaling partnerships is normally required. The main role is to team with other key business partners and global systems integrators to increase revenue and customer success.

Analysis

Prerequisites include analytical skills, partner sales experience, ability to work cross functionally, experience within a B2B Sales environment and knowledgeable about financial services / financial markets.

A bachelor's degree is sometimes required, however, having previous relevant experience in a professional environment tends to be the main priority for employers.

Top Skills

- SQL and Excel
- Sales experience with digital products
- Strong interpersonal skills

Experience

Understanding of financial services sector

Experience corresponding with both potential partners and final clients: presenting the proposition, describing the platform and how that could be an asset for the partners and the end users

Experience in business development / sales

Bachelor's degree or equivalent is preferred

Partner, sales

- ➢ Achieve regional pipeline and revenue targets and other key objectives.
- ➢ Develop a plan to team with other key business partners and global systems integrators to maximise revenue and customer success with alliances.

The Fintech Job Report: Technology is eating finance

Jobs in Fintech and the Required Skills

Partnership Roles

The Fintech Job Report

Partnerships

Essential roles for digital companies

This is a new role that has emerged in banks and Fintech companies. Individuals holding these positions are in charge of helping with customer acquisition or the delivery of a product or service. Typically, they are highly experienced in related roles such as Sales, Marketing or Business Development.

Since this is a relatively new position, little to no formal training is required. Some companies may accept candidates with limited experiences for the more entry-level positions. When it comes to the more senior or managerial position, 2-10 years of experience is desirable. A bachelor's degree in business administration or a similar field is sometimes a prerequisite.

Partnerships roles are essential and with the growth of Fintech industry, the demand for them is growing rapidly as well. Primary responsibilities for these roles might include; developing and executing strategic and referral relationships contributing to the company's growth, identifying new business opportunities aligned with the organisation's short-term and long-term goals, engaging with leads to promote the generation of revenue or identifying M&A targets within the key focus areas and creating recommendation. They are also in charge of continually analysing the market, competitive landscape or industry tends to identify market opportunities for the Fintech company.

Partnerships

HARD SKILLS

- Project/product management
- Experience in technology and industry software such as salesforce
- Business development
- Sales
- Account management

SOFT SKILLS

- Analytical skills
- Cross functional collaboration
- Communication and interpersonal skills

MINDSET

- Team player
- Proactive
- Organisational and planning skills
- Entrepreneurial mindset
- Ability to deal with uncertainty

EXPERIENCE AND INDUSTRY KNOWLEDGE

- Background in marketing, project/product management, business development, sales, account management or similar roles
- Bachelor's degree in business
- A thorough understanding of the Fintech industry and the company's product

Sales Partnership

| Partnerships

Description

A Sale Partnership (representative) maintains and registers leads, while managing partner opportunities. Flawless execution of commercial partnerships is key to the success of young Fintech companies, so a Sales Partnership representative needs to show a remarkable entrepreneurial spirit to build and drive relationships with partners.

Analysis

Previous relevant experience includes sales experience, in particular, within the partner sector. Great communication skills are essential as well as the ability to clearly present the firm's brand. In order to understand and sell the product of the Fintech company, some technical skills may be required. Regional languages constitute to a further advantage.

Top Skills

- Marketing planning
- Partner program management
- Cross-functional collaboration

Experience

- Experience in sales, business development, marketing or entrepreneurship
- Experience in marketing planning
- Experience in strategic planning and implementation
- Understanding of financial services or Fintech sector
- Bachelor's degree or equivalent is preferred in Finance or Sales

Partnerships manager - Sales

- ➢ Initiating and developing commercial relationships with a variety of strategic partners for Adyen
- ➢ Driving partner recommendations and referrals that lead to new business wins
- ➢ Attending partner events to promote Adyen's solutions

The Fintech Job Report: Technology is eating finance

Strategic Partnership

| Partnerships

Description

A Strategic Partnership Manager identifies and builds relationships with partners such as Financial Institutions/ Fintech/Tech with the goal of growing revenue. These partnerships are often targeted and created in strategic sectors for the company. This role is especially crucial for Fintech companies that have a business model that requires a network effect such as platforms.

Analysis

Previous relevant experience includes working for a Financial Institution or a Network with a focus in the B2B market and other Fintech companies that have a focus on B2B. Crucial skills for this position include strong analytical skills, ability to handle complex deals that involve multiple parties as well as relationships/project management.

Top Skills

- Finance experience
- Marketing analytics
- Interpersonal skills

Experience

- Demonstrated and proven sales results
- Experience in financial services or consumer finance
- Experience working in large organisations across different business groups such as marketing, sales, channel, services, development, and product management to drive results
- Experience selling a B2B payment

Marketing Manager, Strategic Partnerships

> Develop and execute collaborative partner marketing campaigns
> Create succinct strategies, plans and tools to enable both our internal sales team and our partner sales team to sell these partnership integrations successfully

The Fintech Job Report: Technology is eating finance

Marketing Partnership

| Partnerships

Description

A Marketing Partnership (representative) leads key growth and consumer brand partnership initiatives as a member of a team, responsible for establishing relationships that grow brand awareness and ultimately customer base. In this role, one works closely with divisions such as Product, Data, Engineering, Marketing and Communications and Sales.

Top Skills

- Brand partnerships
- Marketing planning
- Cross functional work

Analysis

Relevant experience for this role includes Marketing Manager, Brand Partnership Manager and Business Development Strategist in Tech or Consulting, ideally in regulated industries. Deep understanding of the Fintech firms product is also a requirement while crucial skills for this role are communication, leadership and negotiation. An existing strong network of go-to people is often preferred as well as additional languages.

Experience

- Ability to lead multi-stakeholder groups and effectively utilise resources and relationships to drive results
- Experience in payments a plus - comfort and interest in becoming an expert in new industries a must
- Bachelor's degree or equivalent is preferred
- Proven success in both B2B and B2C marketing environments

Senior Manager, Partner Marketing, EMEA

- Work closely with the EMEA sales and field marketing teams to create opportunities and build partner value propositions
- Communicate regularly with partners to inform them of platform updates, promotions or joint marketing resources and education

Jobs in Fintech and the Required Skills

Risk & Compliance Roles

The Fintech Job Report

Risk & Compliance

Essential roles for digital companies

Risk & Compliance plays an important role in companies operating in any industry, including Fintech. This division is responsible for managing risks and aligning the company's operations with any relevant regulatory requirements and policies in the financial industry.

Individuals in these roles should have substantial experiences handling regulatory and legal issues related to Fintech and Financial Services. Additionally, having a strong foundation of legal knowledge and an understanding of regulatory frameworks, licensing and applications, compliance and enforcement matters or privacy and cybersecurity is crucial in making sure that risk is managed appropriately.

Risk & compliance roles typically require a bachelor's degree in Law and about 5-15 years of experience for more senior positions. For entry level roles and internships, an ongoing bachelor's degree is acceptable.

Specific responsibilities for this role include researching regulatory frameworks, monitoring and updating internal policies, KYC and AML policies in line with the relevant regulations, conducting relevant screening for clients and employees, as well as keeping up-to-date with relevant news related to both the regulatory bodies and the Fintech industry.

Risk & Compliance

HARD SKILLS

- AML legislation + regulation
- Database operations
- Finance operations

SOFT SKILLS

- Interpersonal skills
- Business acumen is encouraged
- Cross functional collaboration
- Active listening skills
- Written and verbal communication
- Multi-tasking and time management

MINDSET

- Learner mindset
- Proactive
- Identification and prevention of risk
- Forward thinker
- Analytical and detail oriented

EXPERIENCE AND INDUSTRY KNOWLEDGE

- Experience in different regulatory frameworks both nationally and internationally
- Bachelor's degree in law/ advanced degree such as masters or PhD
- Fintech acumen and knowledge of the regulatory space

Technical Program Manager

| Risk and Compliance

Description

A Technical Product Manager manages cross-functional product security projects while developing and improving Compliance Program documentation procedures. In Fintech companies, one of the roles a Technical Programme Manager holds is to reduce the Compliance burden for Engineers while partnering with cross-functional teams within Engineering, Risk And Compliance, Product and Finance.

Analysis

Relevant experience includes working within regulated environments in security related technical roles. Technical skills include knowledge of cloud infrastructure, coding and various operating systems. Communication and organisational skills are crucial for this role that needs to balance internal engineering processes, business needs, and external audit requirements.

Top Skills

- Product Security experience
- Program management
- Cross functional collaboration

Experience

- Technical program management or similar experience
- Experience in product management or engineering roles preferred
- Solid technical foundation and ability to master new technical concepts and technologies quickly

---

Technical Program Manager, Risk Product

➢ Partner with portfolio analytics team and product managers to reduce the financial risk profile of established products

➢ Manage technology programs and gather project requirements for shipping of impactful and reliable products and platforms

Compliance Officer

| Risk and Compliance

Description

Compliance officers research and communicate compliance standards to ensure that organisation's operations meet them. Other areas of responsibility include but are not limited to: liaison with law enforcement and regulatory agencies, monitoring of prohibited activities and deployment of tools to assess compliance gaps.

Analysis

In Fintech companies, this role is becoming increasingly important given the regulatory pressure of regulators worldwide and it's part in Risk and Compliance. Compared to pure Finance companies, a compliance analyst working in Fintech may work closely with the Engineering or Data department to implement automated compliance tools. Hence, an interest and passion for technology holds great importance.

Top Skills

- **Regulatory regional expertise**
- **Database operations**
- **Investigative skills**

Experience

Experience working with state and/or federal regulators and agencies (i.e., FinCEN)

Certified Anti-Money Laundering Specialist (CAMS) and/or Certified Regulatory Compliance Manager (CRCM)

Economics, accounting, finance, lending, risk

Fraud principles and practices

Senior Compliance Analyst

> ➢ *Review and investigation of escalations in relation to AML, CTF and fraud monitoring as well as potential sanctions violations*
> ➢ *Work with clients to understand their product design and parameters, perform KYB/KYC due diligence, customer onboarding, AML risk assessment*

Risk Intelligence Engineer

| Risk and Compliance

Description

Risk Intelligence Data Engineers assist with the creation of a scalable and sustainable Risk Intelligence Data Architecture to support business requirements. They often interact with the Business Intelligence team to provide insights aimed at developing new business intelligence solutions. In Fintech companies they often work in teams such as Credit, Risk or Compliance.

Analysis

Previous relevant work experience includes working on large scalable database platforms as well as designing and implementing data models specifically for Fintech and Financial Services. Strong technical skills are a strict requirement, moreover good time management and organisational skills. This is typically not an entry level position.

Top Skills

- Big Data tools (Spark, Kafka, Hive, NiFi)
- Database operations
- Proactivity

Experience

- Software engineering experience
- Understanding of data & how to design data models for Payments, Fintech, Financial Services
- Programming with Hadoop, Hive, Scala/Spark, Python and SQL (MPP database, Google Cloud Platform a plus)

Risk Intelligence Engineer

➢ Proposing and implementing product ideas that directly reduce Stripe's risk exposure
➢ Building live Stripe systems that interface with ML models to make risk decisions, and enact interventions and mitigations to protect Stripe from losses

The Fintech Job Report: Technology is eating finance

Privacy & Compliance Engineer

| Risk and Compliance

Description

Privacy and Compliance Engineers implement compliance solutions that may be needed to comply with Data Privacy regulations. This role is common especially in Fintech companies covering Insurance or in environments where Data Privacy rules have been widely implemented.

Top Skills

- Privacy legal frameworks and tech issues
- Security or Privacy experience
- Collaboration

Analysis

This is not an entry level position and requires previous experience in software engineering that allowed for great exposures to a variety of programming languages. Passion for security, privacy and compliance or experience in highly regulated industries are often an advantage. The ability to understand Data Privacy regulations constitutes to an advantage.

Experience

Experience working on privacy solutions in an engineering capacity (e.g. tracker blocker, password manager, or similar technology

Deep understanding of web technologies, how they can be exploited and how they can be used to prevent against exploits

Deep technical understanding of online privacy threats and the existing solution space to protect against them

---

Senior security engineer

➢ *Working with a variety of technologies, and have increasingly impactful accomplishments*
➢ *Using your technical skills to automate and engineer solutions to manual processes, is energising for you*

The Fintech Job Report: Technology is eating finance

Fraud Officer

| Risk and Compliance

Description

Fraud officers investigate cases of frauds (internally or with clients) as well as work with the Product team to implement anti-fraud solutions where relevant. In Fintech companies this is a crucial role to comply with regulations and avoid reputational damages for companies that are typically building up their reputation. In addition, in order to identify fraud efficiently basic coding skills are required to develop automated solutions.

Analysis

Attention to details, communication skill, strong ethical standards and good data analytics abilities are crucial for this role. For this role, relevant experience can be acquired in Banking, or in general, Fraud related roles. Common degrees include Mathematics, Economics, Engineering or Finance.

Top Skills

- Database operations
- Experience with regulatory agencies
- Cross functional collaboration

Experience

- Experienced fraud investigator
- Working knowledge of Cifas and SIRA; and awareness of current fraud trends
- Bachelor's degree or equivalent is preferred in Economics, Maths, Engineering
- Sound technical knowledge of fraud prevention, tools and strategies

Senior Analyst – Fraud

➢ Use statistical analysis tools and techniques to develop automated fraud detection and real time decisioning strategies
➢ Collaborate with date scientists to build and implement fraud pattern models

The Fintech Job Report: Technology is eating finance

AML Officer

| Risk and Compliance

Description

An Anti-Money Laundering officer implements the company AML policy to ensure that the company is not exposed to criminal risk by inadvertently facilitating financial crime. This role, often required by law, is crucial for Fintech companies that often aim to hire experienced AML given that their core business might be easily used with bad intentions.

Analysis

Fintech companies are looking for AML officers with relevant experience in the Finance industry but also capable of implementing automated and data-driven processes. AML officers need to be able to clearly explain AML compliance while developing mitigation strategies.

Communication and critical thinking skills are crucial for this role that is extremely valuable for Fintech companies that are often working with new technology, such as blockchain.

Top Skills

- AML legislation and regulations
- Money laundering expertise
- Communication

Experience

- Experience in an AML-related role or equivalent
- Awareness of financial service firms obligations in respect of financial crime prevention
- Advanced knowledge of relevant AML, CTF, OFAC, ABC and NACHA rules and regulations
- CAMS or other relevant professional qualifications

AML officer

- *Staying up to date on regulatory and policy developments relevant to Fintech*
- *Developing risk assessments, reporting, training and transaction monitoring*
- *Working collaboratively with cross-functional tools to develop creative solutions to complex challenges*

Financial Crime Officer

| Risk and Compliance

Description

Financial Crime Officers identify, assess and mitigate financial crime risks. They assist in the development of mitigation solutions while collaborating with the Compliance officer, Legal Department and Product Management team. As for the Compliance officer, Financial Crime team heads often collaborate with external stakeholders such as Regulators of Government authorities. In Fintech companies this role often requires strong technical skills especially when it comes to databases or Data Analysis.

Analysis

Previous relevant experience includes working for regulated financial institutions within Crimes or Compliance teams while basic programming skills are often a prerequisite. The ability to communicate effectively is also crucial for a role connected with multiple teams within the firm. Good managerial skills is also very important in order to identify and mitigate risks in a timely manner.

Top Skills

- AML legislation and regulations
- Risk Identification Capabilities
- Integrity

Experience

- Worked in other Fintech's or innovative Financial Institutions
- Experience in BSA/AML regulations and Financial Crime Compliance
- Prior transaction monitoring & surveillance investigations experience in anti-money laundering (AML), counter-terrorism, anti-bribery, and/or anti-fraud experience

---

Financial Crime Analyst

➢ Working independently within the AML policy framework to determine priorities and meet deadlines
➢ Keep update of changes to mobile payments industry, financial crime trends and regulatory requirements

Cyber Fraud Investigator

| Risk and Compliance

Description

A Cyber Fraud investigator conducts activities aimed at fighting cyber crimes which could impact clients and employees. These include identifying cyber risks and threats, proactively monitoring potential vulnerabilities, providing enterprise threat analysis and actionable intelligence for enterprise risk education. In Fintech companies, this is a crucial role given that the product is typically hosted in a digital environment.

Analysis

Typically this role requires at least 3 years of relevant experience in the Information Security field, proficiency in data analysis and databases, knowledge of security frameworks, network infrastructure and AML regulations.

Tech skills and the ability to communicate effectively at multiple levels are crucial skills for this role. Due to very frequent cyber-attacks, cyber fraud investigation is a role that helps protect the company reputation and credibility with external stakeholders.

Top Skills

- SQL, Tableau, Excel
- AML legislation and regulations
- Detail-oriented

Experience

- Experience in fraud/AML, internal fraud/insider abuse and cyber crimes
- Ability to apply analytical, technical, statistical and quantitative skills to tackle problems
- Proficiency in extracting and processing data using SQL
- Scripting languages, Excel or Tableau for data visualisation and reporting

---

Internal Fraud Investigator

> Investigate cybercrime, complex fraud/AML, internal fraud/insider abuse, and/or high profile events
> Working with data acquisition and forensic examination
> Working with Advanced data query and analysis skills (SQL, SAS, Teradata, Hadoop...)

The Fintech Job Report: Technology is eating finance

Regulatory Policy Officer

| Risk and Compliance

Description

Regulatory Policy Officers identify compliance obligations based on financial regulations. In certain circumstances, they liaise with external stakeholders such as regulators. Fintech companies often do not have the necessary know-how when it comes to the regulatory environment, hence this role is crucial to their success and competitiveness. In addition, the new business model of Fintech companies generates challenges when it comes to the interpretation of regulations.

Analysis

Previous banking experience is often a strict requirement, while crucial to this role is the ability to think critically, pay attention to details and network with relevant stakeholders. Self-driven individuals are usually preferred especially given the dynamic nature of Fintech firms.

Top Skills

- Regulatory frameworks
- Financial services knowledge
- Communication skills

Experience

- Financial licensing, AML, CTF and Sanctions
- Subject matter expert in regulatory processes, laws and regulations
- Experience of both the informal and formal aspects of how regulatory policy is shaped and developed
- Experience in a fast paced environment

Regulatory Compliance Officer

➢ *Identify compliance obligations based on financial obligation*
➢ *Translate identified obligations into relevant policies and procedures*
➢ *Represent compliance and regulatory to establish regulatory strategies that align with global objectives*

Jobs in Fintech and the Required Skills

Core Business Finance Roles

The Fintech Job Report

Core Business Finance

Essential roles for digital companies

The Core Business Finance section encompasses jobs that can be typically found in traditional financial institutions. These roles are directly involved in the core activities of the Fintech company. This is a broad category, and the types of roles vary based on the type of the organisation and their specific operations (insurance, payments, banking, wealth management...). Surprisingly, based on our research, there are not a lot of core business finance roles in Fintech, especially in comparison to the more technical roles such as engineering. Technology has automated and replaced a lot of key financial processes and therefore, not as many people are required to handle these types of tasks.

On average, these are not many entry level positions and they require some experience in the same comparable role. Graduate roles and internships are very rare as at least 2 years of experience in the same or comparable role is necessary. A bachelor's degree in finance, accounting, economics, mathematics, business or an equivalent course is a common prerequisite.

As mentioned above, core business finance position are quite rare in Fintech, there are definitely more opportunities of this nature in traditional financial institutions, both when it comes to more junior and senior positions. However, if one wishes to transition from Finance to Fintech, the skills and knowledge required to perform these tasks are very similar, if not the same. A successful candidate will have to showcase a strong passion and interest in Fintech and the specific sector in which that organisation operates.

Specific requirements will vary; however, having a strong fundamental knowledge of financial concepts is mandatory. A strong foundation in mathematics and statistics is also a common prerequisite and a proficiency in Microsoft Excel is a basic requirement for most. Finally, commercial awareness, customer service skills and excellent communication as well as presentation skills are highly valued in these positions.

Core Business Finance

HARD SKILLS

- Microsoft Office Suite (especially Excel and Powerpoint)
- Data Analysis
- Financial Modelling and Analysis
- Statistics and Mathematics
- R, Python, SQL
- Theoretical knowledge of finance

SOFT SKILLS

- Customer service
- Excellent verbal and written communication with internal and external stakeholders
- Good team working and collaborations skills
- Presentations

MINDSET

- Customer-centricity
- Commercial and business awareness
- Analytical thinking
- Problem solving

EXPERIENCE

- Previous experience in a similar role
- Formal education: university degree in Finance, Accounting, Statistics or equivalent (Bachelor's and sometimes Master's degree)
- Fintech and business acumen

Portfolio Analyst

| Core Business Finance

Description

Portfolio analysts are typically proficient in multiple skills such as asset management, trading or risk management. This is a highly analytical and quantitative role that revolve around constructing, managing and optimising investment portfolios based on financial models and analyses. Client relationship management and presenting them with portfolio performance reports are also common aspects of the job.

Analysis

This is a position that usually requires previous experience in asset management or an equivalent role. Due to the nature of the job, a portfolio analyst should have a strong financial and data analysis skills, as well as a strong understanding of economics and market trends.

Typically, a bachelor's or master's degree in Economics or Finance is required. Finally, to successfully interact with clients, effective verbal and written communication skills are highly valuable.

Top Skills

- **Financial modeling and data analysis**
- **Verbal and written communication**
- **Commercial awareness**

Experience

- Experience with financial markets
- Financial modeling and analysis
- Data analytics
- Understanding of financial theories and an ability to apply them
- Strong business and commercial acumen
- Bachelor's or Master's degree in Finance, Economics or any other equivalent related areas

---

Portfolio Analyst

➢ *Manage crypto index investment portfolios*
➢ *Portfolio construction based on data driven research and analysis*
➢ *Conduct trade execution, risk management and monitoring of investment portfolios*

The Fintech Job Report: Technology is eating finance

Credit Analyst

| Core Business Finance

Description

Credit analysts asses customers' credit applications and make decisions based on their findings. To conduct their tasks, they need to follow established credit policies, company guidelines and be familiar with any relevant regulatory requirements.

Credit analysts might also be responsible for any communication with the customer as well as verifying any relevant information to the application.

Analysis

The role of a credit analyst is rarely an entry-level position and requires some previous professional experience in the same or equivalent job. This is a highly analytical position and proficiency in Microsoft Excel is a minimum requirement. Knowledge of other data analysis tools such as SQL is highly desirable. Furthermore, due to the customer-centric nature of the position, good communication skills is very important.

Top Skills

- Microsoft Excel
- Data analysis (SQL)
- Lending regulations

Experience

- Experience in a similar position related to credit, loan processing, lending...
- Proficiency in Microsoft Office (Excel in particular)
- Experience using data analysis tools (SQL)
- A strong understanding of lending regulations in the relevant geographical region(s)

Credit Verification Analyst

➢ Perform consumer loan processing activities
➢ Determine the correct decision with an acceptable amount of minimal errors as it relates to the established credit policy
➢ Communicate with clients to verify personal information

Underwriter

| Core Business Finance

Description

Underwriters are responsible for assessing the risk of a specific party as well as determining if they want to take up such risk and under what conditions. This role is quite common in Insurtech companies where underwriters assess insurance policies and consider applicants based on the likelihood of a claim being made. Underwriters can be found in other Fintech sectors as well, for example, credit underwriters conduct detailed research to determine the creditworthiness of applicants.

Analysis

In Fintech companies, this is typically not an entry-level position, as 1-2 years of professional experience is required. Underwriting is a highly quantitative role, so being able to demonstrate strong mathematical and statistical skills is important. A degree in Accounting, Finance, Statistics or Mathematics can be an asset, however, it is rarely a prerequisite of underwriting positions in Fintech. Moreover, good verbal communication skills and customer-centricity are highly desirable.

Top Skills

- **Mathematics and statistics**
- **Data analysis**
- **Customer service**

Experience

- Experience working in a similar role and industry (e.g. Insurance)
- Experience analysing data
- Experience in a fast-growing and fast-moving company
- Written and oral communication
- Degree in Accounting, Finance, Economics, Statistics, Mathematics or equivalent

---

Underwriting Analyst

➢ Assess business model risk and determine credit risk exposure
➢ Prepare concise oral and written summary recommendations
➢ Analyse financial, bank and processing statements to assess credit worthiness

The Fintech Job Report: Technology is eating finance

Fraud Analyst

| Core Business Finance

Description

This is a customer-facing role that can mostly be found in Paytech companies. A fraud analyst focuses on reviewing transactions, identifying any fraudulent activities and implementing processes that mitigate these events based on pre-identified patterns of risk.

For some companies, this role might be more centred around educating merchants on how to use the risk and fraud assessment tools that the company has developed.

Analysis

As computer programmes and tools are used to conduct fraud and risk analysis tasks, having a technical background is highly valued. A degree from a quantitative course such as Statistics, Finance, Computer Science or Engineering is a typical requirement. It is important to note that this role is not very common in Fintech companies, as a lot of the processes around Risk and Fraud assessment are automated, therefore, not as many people are needed to oversee these activities.

Top Skills

- SQL, R, Python
- Knowledge of AML
- Data visualisation: Tableau, Power BI

Experience

- Experience working in a similar role in fraud or risk management
- Experience working in Fintech or strong interest in the field
- Experience dealing with customers
- Working with large data sets
- Working in a fast-paced environment
- Degree: quantitative or technical subjects

Payments Fraud Manager

- Detect Fraud Trends related to Payment schemes and money transfers
- Use data management tools to create modules able to predict, detect and prevent fraud
- Interact with internal and external stakeholders to apply the best fraud prevention solutions

N26

Treasury Analyst

| Core Business Finance

Description

Treasury analysts oversee cash management, funding, foreign exchange or financial management activities of their organisation. This is a highly quantitative role which revolves around analysing and interpreting financial data, forecasts, preparing and presenting reports and developing cash and asset management strategies. Specifically when it comes to Fintech companies, this role is the most relevant to challenger banks.

Analysis

Previous work experience in Finance, or specifically Treasury, is required. A bachelor's or master's degree in Finance, Accounting or Business Administration is a common prerequisite. In terms of skills, the ideal candidate should demonstrate a deep understanding of financial analysis and forecasting tools, as well as good written and oral communication skills.

Top Skills

- **Microsoft Office (Excel, Powerpoint)**
- **Written and oral communication**
- **Financial analysis**

Experience

- Work experience in finance or treasury
- Financial analysis and forecasting
- Proficiency in Microsoft Office (particularly Excel and PowerPoint)
- Strong theoretical knowledge of finance and mathematics
- Bachelor's degree in Finance, Accounting, Business or equivalent (Master's degree is a plus)

Corporate Treasury Analyst

➢ *Manage banking and payer relationships*
➢ *Monitor bank fees and other fund transfer costs*
➢ *Ensure Treasury activities are in compliance with internal and external policies and guidelines*

The Fintech Job Report: Technology is eating finance

Claims Specialist

| Core Business Finance

Description

Claims specialists are responsible for evaluating the circumstances of claims in Insurtech companies. Typical tasks include ensuring that claims are accurately processed and paid as well as managing relationships with users by resolving questions and concerns. More senior individuals such as Claims managers are also in charge of shaping the claims handling strategy of the company.

Analysis

Depending on the seniority of the position, prior claims or general insurance experience might be required. For more senior and advanced positions a bachelor's degree may be required, although, typically only a high school diploma or equivalent is sufficient.

Strong verbal communication and investigative skills are also common must-haves. Finally, proficiency with the Microsoft Office Suite and overall PC literacy are highly desirable.

Top Skills

- Microsoft Office Suite
- Investigation and problem solving
- Communication and customer service

Experience

- Previous claim or insurance experience
- Structuring problems and identifying solutions
- Knowledge of claims handling procedures
- Customer service
- Minimum high school diploma (bachelor's degree required for more managerial positions)

Claims Specialist

- Review claims submitted by members and ensure they are accurately processed and paid
- Answering questions, resolving concerns, and following up with members as necessary

Actuary

| Core Business Finance

Description

This is a role that can most commonly be found in Insurtech companies. Actuaries measure risk and uncertainty of future events as well as their financial consequences. Through the use of various statistical models and actuarial techniques, they identify and adjust for appropriate premiums, losses or expenses policies. The tasks of an actuary often overlap with underwriters, accountants or other finance divisions.

Analysis

Typically, a higher-level education in a quantitative discipline is necessary. Being an associate or in the process of becoming an associate of IFoa or an equivalent actuarial organisation is a common requirement. This is a role that requires strong numerical and technical skills, so knowledge of R, Python, SQL as well as statistical modeling softwares are crucial.

Top Skills

- **Strong Mathematics skills**
- **R, Python, SQL**
- **Statistical modeling, actuarial techniques**

Experience

- Insurance experience in actuary
- Mathematics and statistics
- Experience using R, Python or other modelling software
- IFoA associate or equivalent
- Degree in Mathematics, Science, Engineering, or any other relevant quantitative discipline

---

Actuarial Analyst

➢ *Use statistical models to develop rating plans and recommendations for pricing improvements*
➢ *Build monitoring and reporting on new market metrics vs strategic goals*
➢ *Evaluate and analyse market data to make competitive strategic decisions*

The Fintech Job Report: Technology is eating finance

Conclusion

The development of the Fintech industry is now a trend that is well entrenched and is likely to continue with the digitalisation of financial services.

For those looking for new careers, this is a sector that combines high growth, competitive salaries, and an interesting career progression. In addition, it is a part of the wider finance industry, with potential to move between verticals such as banking, insurance or asset management.

Despite these attractive features, the Fintech industry finds it challenging to recruit the right talents, not because of a lack of candidates, but a lack of qualified candidates. On the other hand, many professionals with the right skills are not aware of the opportunities in Fintech, or do not realise that their skills are easily transferable in this dynamic industry.

This is a lost opportunity both for Fintech employers who cannot find the talents needed to help them grow, and for candidates who cannot benefit from well-paid jobs with potential for career progression.

There is an opportunity for the industry to solve this mismatch by increasing the awareness and understanding of Fintech, for example with initiatives such as this report, but also at the level of universities and professional bodies. At the level of individuals, a better understanding of the industry and the job landscape of Fintech would help those in need of upskilling or reskilling to properly focus their efforts on what is required for their desired position.

At the end of the day, the importance of Fintech jobs exceeds the limited world of the industry, but is ultimately a predictor of how jobs in financial services will evolve as the whole industry becomes digital. This has therefore special resonance not only for Fintech employees, but also those working in financial services, banks, insurers, and the wider industry.

Ultimately, there is an opportunity for the whole industry, financial institutions, governments, policymakers and regulators to focus their efforts on building talents and skills which are adapted to the new world of financial services.

Appendix

The Fintech Job Report

▶ **Report Methodology**

▶ **List of Contributors**

The Appendix

Report Methodology

The Fintech Job Report

The Identification of 225 Fintech Unicorns

As of 1st October 2021, we have been able to identify 225 Fintech Unicorns, companies whose valuations exceed $1 billion. CFTE's definition of Fintech is "the impact that technology has on transforming the financial industry". Due to our broad definition, our list includes a variety of organisations: smaller and early-stage Fintech startups, established startups such as Stripe, but also large payment companies such as Visa or Tech companies like Ant Financial. We have decided to include these companies as they fit the general profile of Fintech in terms of not only activities, but also their ratio of market capitalisation to number of employees. They have significantly fewer employees in comparison to their counterparts in the traditional finance industry – a characteristic typical for Fintech and Tech. Our research shows that on average, the top 40 banks employ 130,000 people, whilst Mastercard, Visa and Ant Financial only have between 10,000 and 20,000 each.

For listed companies, we used Google Finance to identify and update their market capitalisation, whilst the data for private companies was sourced from press releases and news articles. It is important to note that private valuations are difficult to compare (due to preferential rights, etc.) and disclosed numbers can have inaccuracies. Some organisations have not been included in our analysis as there were no valuations public at the time of the report's release.

Creating a Taxonomy for Fintech Jobs

Our preliminary analysis found more than 40,000 job openings in the top 225 Fintech companies from which we extracted over 100 of the most common roles in the industry. Up until now, there has not been an official taxonomy for jobs in Fintech and therefore, a new categorisation system was created. We divided the roles into **14 job families**, which can be further classified into **3 distinct categories**:

1. **Generic**: roles found in most organisations in any industry (e.g., Human Resources, Legal)
2. **Technology**: technical and non-technical roles most commonly found in Tech companies (e.g., Engineering, Marketing & Communications)
3. **Finance**: roles typically found in traditional financial institutions (Risk & Compliance and Core Business Finance)

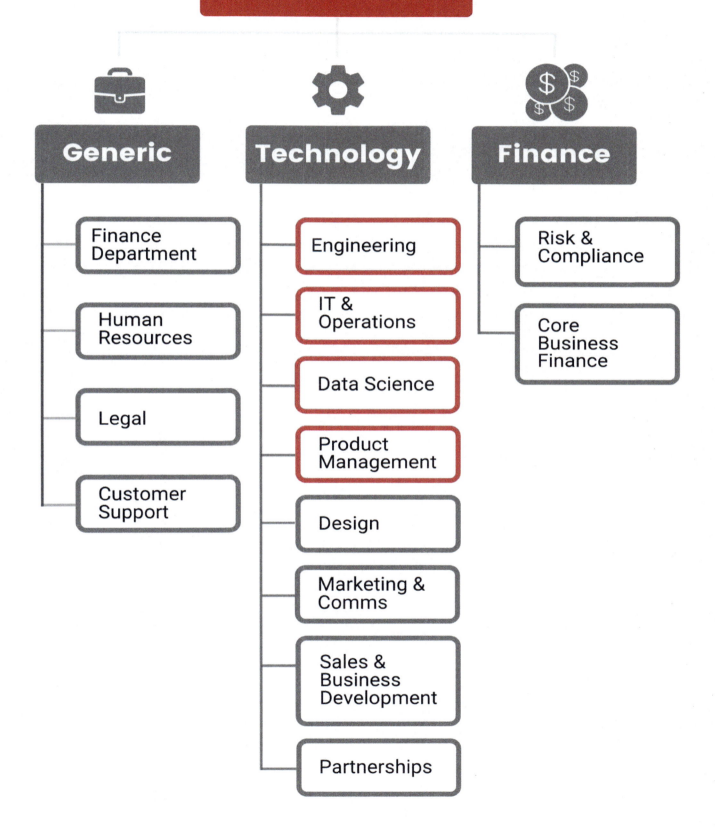

The Fintech Job Report only covers the 60 roles of Technology and Finance companies, as reports analysing jobs such as HR or Legal are already in place.

Once the Fintech job taxonomy was created, we analysed each role, extracted the most common requirements and identified the job description, the necessary hard skills, soft skills, mindset, experience and industry knowledge to provide an insight into the most common jobs in Fintech.

Mapping the Fintech Job Market

To gain a better understanding of the Fintech job market worldwide, we identified the aggregate number of employees and job postings per each continent. To find the number of employees, a combination of company reports and LinkedIn was used. For job postings, our main source of information were career portals and LinkedIn as well. In instances when we were unable to find any accurate public data, we reached out to company representatives and acquired the necessary information in this manner.

The Appendix

Contributors

The Fintech Job Report

Content and Research

Huy Nguyen Trieu
Co-Founder

Ines Ouali
Fintech Research Analyst

Guido Bassi
Fintech Research Analyst

Kabeer Chauhan
Fintech Research Analyst

Waridah Makena
Fintech Research Analyst

Michaela Do
Fintech Research Analyst

Sarah Khan
Fintech Research Analyst

Design and Marketing

Paul Putscher
Marketing Lead

Urvi Bhatia
Marketing Associate

Irina Barzykina
Fintech Analyst

Printed in Great Britain
by Amazon